PERIOD-STYLE
FLOWERS

PERIOD-STYLE
FLOWERS
Flower Arranging Projects inspired by the Past

SARAH PEPPER

SPECIAL PHOTOGAPHY BY DAVID GARNER

THE NATIONAL TRUST

First published in 2004 by National Trust Enterprises Ltd
36 Queen Anne's Gate, London SW1H 9AS

www.nationaltrust.org.uk

Cataloguing in Publication Data is available from the
British Library

ISBN 07078 0374 8

Designed by Fiona Roberts

Colour reproduction by Digital Imaging Ltd

Printed and bound in China

Photographic credits
All the flower projects were taken by David Garner.
The historic interiors and details are from the National
Trust Photographic Library: Peter Aprahamian, p.115
(below); Bill Batten, pp. 34, 53; Michael Caldwell,
pp. 112, 115 (above); Andreas von Einsiedel, pp 16
(below), 35, 36, 37, 51, 81, 82 (above), 83, 113; John
Hammond, pp.14, 15, 16 (above), 52; Nadia Mackenzie,
pp.17, 50, 82 (below); James Mortimer, p.114.
Front cover: Elizabethan-style tussie mussie using
lavender, pink roses, red spray roses, anemones,
penstemon, escallonia, santolina, rosemary, bay
and berries.
Back cover: Stuart-style garland (see pp. 42-3)
Frontispiece: Georgian-style formal table arrangement
(see pp. 60-3)

Contents

Acknowledgements

I would like to give heartfelt thanks to a veritable army of people who have been instrumental in the creation of this book. To my lovely clients who have encouraged me and my flower-arranging business since its first faltering steps. To many of the National Trust's staff, especially Denise Melhuish, Christina Le Fey and the marvellous team at Killerton House. To my publisher and editor Margaret Willes for her firm judgement and wonderful contributions to the historical content in the chapter openers, and to her sorcerer's apprentice, Andrew Cummins. To Fiona Roberts, the book's ever-patient designer, and to David Garner, a truly gifted photographer with soothing words and an emergency stash of chocolate – a rare blend indeed! To Andrew Stanistreet, his assistant and the ladies of the reception area at Wedgwood & Co. for arranging loan and despatch of so many beautiful containers. To dear friends and family, especially long- suffering parents whose gardens I regularly denude. To Sarah, my still, small voice of calm. To Brenda's unflagging support, Kathleen's unconditional acceptance of wailing and gnashing of teeth, and to Uncle Dicky's remarkable nippers.

And last, but by no means least, to my husband Christopher for his customary blend of stoical good humour, gentle persuasion, unparalleled hospitality and epicurean masterpieces. This book is testament to his unique gifts which weave their special magic behind the scenes.

Sarah Pepper, September 2003

Introduction

This project was prompted by my fascination for social history combined with an all-consuming passion for flower arranging that was probably inspired by my late grandmother. She influenced the planting and layout of the garden from which I still regularly cut.

For a number of years now I have enjoyed a special relationship with the National Trust which has led me to teaching flower arranging and traditional crafts at numerous properties, designing and arranging floral decorations for 'every day' displays and special celebrations and generally advising on historical styles of floral decorations. I am delighted that such a widespread interest in period-style floral decorations continues to thrive and hope that this book will be a useful tool for the many eager flower arrangers who have expressed a need for a working handbook.

Throughout history the individual needs of households have evolved, as have the gardens which supported them and, just as our ancestors would have adapted fashions, recipes and decorations to their resources and means, so do we today. Not all of the arrangements in this book will appeal to you, but do experiment with different varieties of flowers available for that period until you find combinations that last well in your environment and, hopefully, give an overall style that you can live with.

I have based the designs for this book on details from paintings, diarist's notes and publications of each period which, inevitably, mainly recorded the lives of high status families. In lesser households the high fashion of the day would have probably gone largely unnoticed, with the occupants having to 'make do and mend', probably following long-held traditions and with reluctance towards change born of financial necessity. It would appear that the Victorians could well have been responsible for beginning the British fascination with 'DIY', as for the first time widely available periodicals offered tasteful decorating solutions for those on a budget and books suggested appropriate hobbies and decorations for ladies of the new, and rapidly rising, middle classes.

left: Tussie mussie using red spray roses, orange roses, anemones, rose hips, lady's mantle, lavender, rosemary, conifer, bay and sedum.

The book is divided into chapters devoted to five different periods in history, namely Elizabethan, Stuart, Georgian, Victorian and Edwardian, and their styles of floral decoration. Each chapter opens with a collage of flowers that, to me, encapsulate that period. This is followed by an introduction to each, seeking to capture the social and stylistic history of the time, using some of the interiors of houses that now belong to the National Trust. These introductions should help to put into context the developments in flower arranging affecting that specific period.

Next comes a section dealing with appropriate containers. I am sure that you are not all proud possessors of seventeenth-century delftware bough pots or Victorian urns; and even if you were, would not want to risk using them for your arrangements. Therefore I have recommended the shapes and styles of containers rather than sticking accurately to historical examples. After this section comes easy to follow, step-by-step re-creations of traditional arrangements with explanations of how they would have been made and where they would have been displayed in the home. I have tried to provide as wide a spread as possible for these, to include arrangements that can be displayed at all times, and some for special occasions, including Christmas and weddings.

It has often been said that fashion takes approximately one hundred years to turn full circle and many modern styles of decorations have their roots firmly in the past. A vast selection of 'antique containers' are totally relevant to today's genres of flower arranging and still have a useful place in our homes.

As I arrange flowers in an old blue and white jug for a windowsill in my sitting room, I like to think that I am enjoying the scent and colours of flowers which have been valued by generations before me, and that I am carrying on a tradition that firmly links me to the past.

I am confident that the step-by-step projects in this book can be achieved by complete beginners as well as more seasoned flower arrangers, who may adapt projects to their own favourite methods of arranging. Above all, I hope that this book provides you with the inspiration and confidence to enjoy arranging flowers for yourself, friends and family, and visitors.

Practical advice

Choosing your Flowers and Foliage

If you are cutting materials from your own garden, try to avoid the hottest part of the day. Plan to cut in the early morning or evening when the plants will have a better chance not to wilt. If you have to cut flowers and foliage on a very hot day, try to carry a small bucket with a few centimetres/inches of water around the garden, into which you can pop the stems as soon as they are cut. This will give them a much better chance of survival.

Try to choose a mixture of budded, partially open and fully open blooms to give balance to your arrangements. Be prepared to replace the fully open blooms before they are truly past their best. However, if you are making your arrangement well in advance of when it is needed, then choose more budded stems, but be aware that your arrangement will considerably change in look overall as the flowers mature and open.

How to save some of your Holly Berries from the Birds

You may be happy to share some of your lovely berries with the birds, but it is always useful to ensure that you will have some for decorating at Christmas. Pick some good stems in late November or early December and cut the base of the stems at a sharp 45° angle to allow more moisture to be drawn up. Stand these stems in a bucket of damp sand, remembering to keep the sand damp. If you use a bucket of water, it will get very smelly and stagnant. Throw an old towel over the berries to keep off the frost – and persistent birds – and stand the bucket in a sheltered part of the garden (or better still, in the garage or shed). Your holly berries should still be looking crisp and fresh ready to use at Christmas.

Conditioning Flowers and Foliage

Conditioning means cutting the stems of flowers and foliage (preferably at a sharp 45° angle so as to allow greater moisture absorption), removing all lower foliage so that it does not sit below the water line and encourage the growth of bacteria, and putting the stems into tepid water for a minimum of four hours. Stand your bucket of flowers and foliage in a cool room, out of direct sunlight.

Glossy or waxy foliage, such as ivy, camellia, rhododendrons, can benefit from being submerged under water for a few hours. This will not only condition the foliage but is also useful as it cleans off any cobwebs or dirt – particularly useful for long stems of trailing ivy. Never submerge grey, silver or fluffy foliage, as it will not absorb the water, but merely rot.

Pre-conditioning Flower and Foliage

Not all flowers and foliage require pre-conditioning, and if you are working on a large project with a quantity of materials, you may not have the time or inclination to pre-condition each stem.

Always strip cellophane or paper from flowers bought from florists or supermarkets as soon as you get them home. Many fleshy stemmed flowers tend to sweat inside cellophane if the weather is hot.

For woody stems, take a knife and carefully strip back the bark from the bottom 5cm/2ins of stem and then make a slit of at least 5cm/2ins into the base of the stem, as this will allow it to take up a greater amount of water.

Prolonging the Life of your Flowers

Always remember to keep your arrangements topped up with water at least every other day during warm weather. You may find it useful to mist spray them with water every day, situation permitting, or even remove them to a cooler room overnight where it is more appropriate for you to mist them with water.

Try to remove from your arrangement any flowers that are damaged or fading, as these stems give off ethylene gases which will make your healthy flowers fade all the faster. Fruit also gives off ethylene gas as it ripens, so don't expect arrangements with fruit and flowers to last in tip-top condition for very long.

Cleaning Containers

All containers, including buckets, greatly benefit from a good clean with a non-abrasive scourer and a small amount of environmentally friendly bleach at least once a week. This will help to keep your glassware sparkling but also inhibit the growth of bacteria and algae in your containers.

That horribly slimy sheen won't be removed by just a slosh around with clean water!

Changing the water in vases and containers every other day will not only keep the flowers fresher and limit any unpleasant smells, but also avoids visibly murky water, a tell-tale sign of old flowers.

Cleaning Scissors and Secateurs

Keeping scissors and secateurs clean will limit the chance of spreading disease from one plant to another when cutting your garden plants.

The Easy Way to make Wired Bows

Take a piece of ribbon and fold it into a collar (as though you were putting a scarf around your neck). Take the point at which the ribbon meets as it crosses and ruche the centre of the bow together as if you were pleating the fabric. Make

TIPS

One metre (one yard) of ribbon will make one large, two medium or three very small bows. If, however, you are using wide ribbon, it will be quite difficult to make three bows from this length.

a small hook on the end of a piece of stub wire. Place this hook on the centre of the bow and wire it firmly together. Have a go – it really is that easy once you acquire the knack.

Wiring Fir Cones

Turn the fir cone upside down so that the base faces you, take a firm stub wire and hold the end of the wire underneath the lowest open part of the cone. With your other hand run the rest of the wire around the base of the cone under the 'leaves' of the cone, leaving a length of the wire ready for securing the cone later. The wire will disappear inside the leaves and stay invisible when you turn the cone upright.

Wiring Walnuts

Turn the walnut upside down and at the base of the shell there will be a tiny cross where the halves of the shell meet. Push a stub wire into this cross and you will find that it is completely soft so that the wire passes easily inside the shell. You may want to put some glue onto the end of the wire to ensure that it stays within the shell.

Gilding Fir Cones

To gild cones, or any other foliage, seed heads or flowers, try a bright gold aerosol spray, as sprays that are categorised as antique gold can look very muddy when used on a dark base colour, such as deep brown fir cones. Give the aerosol a good shake, then lightly waft the spray over the wired cones until you are happy with the effect. With flowers or foliage, I would recommend moving the foliage/flowers into the spray to avoid blobs of paint and a heavily clogged look. It can be useful to hold the cones inside a recycled cardboard box to avoid any damage to surrounding furnishings, and always remember to use the aerosol in a well-ventilated area.

ELIZABETHAN DISPLAY

The Elizabethans (1558-1603) did not suffer from false modesty. Those with status or wealth – and preferably a combination of both – would display it on every occasion. Elizabeth Hardwick, known as Bess of Hardwick, gained both status and wealth through her four marriages and at her death, aged over eighty, she was one of the richest women in England. The Elizabethan love of display can clearly be seen at Hardwick Hall in Derbyshire, the house that Bess built in the 1590s at the death of her fourth husband, the Earl of Shrewsbury.

Wealth enabled her to build a great house on the top of a hill, with huge windows that reflect the rays of the sun like a lantern. The interior was lavishly furnished with tapestries, heavy furniture, plasterwork friezes and elaborate chimneypieces. Status was established by placing all the state rooms on the top floor, so that honoured guests would climb the great staircase that meanders through the house, eventually reaching the

above: Velvet panel decorated with silver strapwork and floral sprigs, with the monogram 'ES' for Elizabeth Shrewsbury (Bess of Hardwick) and the Hardwick stag.

High Great Chamber where Bess would greet them seated below a canopy of state.

Elizabethan life was intensely hierarchical. Between 1559 and 1597, Elizabeth I issued a series of proclamations known as sumptuary laws, stipulating the furs, fabrics and trimmings that could be worn by certain ranks of society. Even colours came in for scrutiny. One commentator wrote in 1577 of how the Englishman used to wear his 'coat, gown and cloak of brown-blue or puke [blue-black] ... and a doublet of sad tawny [dark orange brown] or black velvet or other comely silk, without such cuts and garish colours as are worn in these days and never brought in but by the consent of the French, who think themselves the gayest men when they have most diversities of jags and change of colours about them'.

Puke and sad tawny were just two of the wonderful names given to colour tones by the Elizabethans. Reds, for instance, ranged from rich 'lustie gallant' to pale 'maiden's blush'. One of the favourite reds chosen for rich bedhangings was carnation, which was often combined with gold for maximum effect. At Canons Ashby in Northamptonshire, Sir Erasmus Dryden commissioned decorative paintings to commemorate his ancestors and family connections for his Winter Parlour in the 1590s (see p.16). Recently revealed, they show how the Elizabethans loved strong colours, especially reds, that would have glowed in candlelight.

Colours carried with them a language of their own. White represented chastity, and the Queen expected her maids of honour to wear white and silver at court, and to live up to their colours. Yellow represented hope, joy and forgiveness, but yellow-red stood for deception. Green, with its association with fertility, was the colour of love, but turquoise stood for jealousy. Red was associated with courage, and Mary Queen of Scots donned a crimson petticoat to face the executioner's axe.

This love of allusion also applied to flowers. The Elizabethans inherited the religious associations with flowers from their pre-Reformation ancestors, but added to these classical references and, at the court of Elizabeth, virginal connotations. The High Great Chamber at

right: Detail from the plasterwork frieze in the High Great Chamber at Hardwick Hall, Derbyshire, showing Diana the huntress and some of her attendants.

Hardwick is decorated by an elaborate plaster frieze depicting Diana the huntress in a forest glade, surrounded by her ladies, exotic animals and flowers. The connection being drawn is between Diana, the virgin huntress, and Elizabeth, the virgin queen. The flowers have been chosen to maintain this connection: lilies, the flowers of purity, the foxglove or 'virgin's fingers', pinks, which the herbalist Gerard called 'virgin-like' and the florentine iris.

Bess also commissioned a portrait of Elizabeth I which still hangs in the Long Gallery at Hardwick. The Queen is depicted wearing an elaborate dress decorated with fabulous sea monsters and flowers. It's difficult to tell whether these have been embroidered or stained (painted) onto her skirt. The decoration on this dress is not merely for show: it is full of 'conceits' or distilled images concealing a complex meaning. The swan, for instance, symbolises female beauty – in contrast to the spouting whale and the ferocious dragon-like creature. Here again, too, are the flowers that send a message – the cornflower, the white eglantine rose, the viola, and, rising proudly between the royal feet, the iris.

At Hardwick there are also Bess's textiles to give us an idea of the kinds of flowers favoured by the Elizabethans. Against rich red backgrounds, her embroidered cushions and hangings show the eglantine rose, another flower associated with chastity, the marigold, honeysuckle, cornflowers and a rare early sighting of the tulip.

Another excellent source are paintings of the period. A portrait of Sir Thomas More and his family provides an idea of the kind of flowers that were popular in the sixteenth century and how they were arranged and used to decorate homes. The group portrait, originally painted by Hans Holbein c.1526, has disappeared, but a copy was made some time in the 1590s, and can be seen at Nostell Priory in Yorkshire. Most of the flowers shown are native British plants, but the peony in one of the arrangements is not recorded in cultivation in England until 1594.

I have reproduced one of the arrangements from the More family portrait on page 18 to show the kind of containers that are appropriate for the style of this period. The overall style is simple, using a mixture of varieties of flowers, often including wild ones. With little furniture in the centre of the room, floral decorations would have been mainly displayed on window sills, or standing on the floor or filling the fireplace during the summer months. Scent was a very important part of any floral decoration, and useful in masking the unpleasant odours that Elizabethans had to endure daily. The projects that I have included in this chapter all had the dual function of fragrance and beauty.

right: Portrait of Elizabeth I, painted in the 1590s, in the Long Gallery at Hardwick Hall.

left: The Winter Parlour at Canons Ashby, Northamptonshire, showing the brilliant colours of the crests that decorate the top of the walnut panelling.

right: The canopy of state in the High Great Chamber at Hardwick Hall, with the plasterwork frieze of Diana above.

Elizabethan containers

IN THE SIXTEENTH century there were no specific containers for the arrangement of flowers, apart from the bough (or bow) pot in which large stems or even branches could be displayed. Contemporary descriptions of 'flower pots' seem to cover a variety of vases, pots and bowls, including even large, urn-shaped containers with two handles. It is safe to say that any domestic container would have been used to display stems of wild flowers picked from the hedgerows or fields.

Only wealthy and high status households could have afforded specific containers for the display of cut flowers or plants. Blue and white porcelain was extremely rare: Bess of Hardwick, for instance, had her precious Ming vase mounted in silver-gilt. Blue and white glazed earthenware imitations of oriental china, known as delftware, were more common. Containers with narrow necks were used for single blooms or simple sprays.

Blue and white bough pot

Blue and white bowl

left: A recreation of one of the flower arrangements in the late sixteenth-century portrait of Sir Thomas More and his family, using a metal ewer with stems of monkshood, pinks, golden rod, veronica, cornflowers, pansies, a longiforum lily and sweet Williams.

Pewter ewer

Glazed earthenware bough pot

Blue and white china cache pot

Glazed earthenware pot

Wooden pot pourri box
with pierced lid

Pewter goblet

Tussie mussies

pink spray roses
pink sweet peas
lady's mantle *(protection)*
lime blossom
valerian
periwinkle
myrtle *(love)*
mint *(virtue)*
rosemary *(remembrance)*
sage *(domestic virtue)*
ivy *(fidelity)*
1 metre *(1 yard)* pink ribbon
1 metre *(1 yard)* white ribbon
floral tape

TUSSIE MUSSIES, or nosegays, were fragrant posies of herbs and flowers often used to sweeten foul air and ward off disease. Their aromatic properties were even thought to provide protection from risk of the plague.

The herbs and flowers chosen to make up the tussie mussie could convey a specific message from the giver to the recipient. I have listed some of the meanings that the Elizabethans gave. These often differ from the list of the 'language of flowers' on pages 136 to 141, because the Victorians developed this into a new art form, subtly changing the symbolism of many ancient plants to fit with their fashions for colour, scent and desirability.

You may find it useful to think in terms of an hour-glass figure when making the tussie mussie: ie, that the stems cross in a nipped waist and flare out at the base. This will give you a loose and more natural feel to the top of the nosegay, following the Elizabethan style. If all your stems are held together in an upright fashion, you will end up with a posy more in the Georgian style.

If your hands begin to ache while you are adding each 'collar' of the materials, take some floral tape and bind each layer to keep the posy tightly together. This will be especially helpful if it is to be carried by an exuberant recipient!

Your tussie mussie should stay fresh for up to a week if left in water. If you are making it for a gift or special occasion, you can easily prepare it the day before, leaving off the ribbons, and put it into a glass of water. Remove from the water at least an hour before you need it, dry the base of the stems with a towel and tie on the ribbons. Stand the tussie mussie back upright in a dry glass, avoiding resting it on one side for too long to prevent a flattened edge.

Tussie mussies are surprisingly easy to dry. All you have to do is hang them upside down in a well-ventilated place that is out of direct sunlight (the sunlight would bleach the colour out of the flowers before they actually dried). In the summer, you may well be able to dry your tussie mussie in about two weeks. As your flowers and foliage will shrink slightly as they dry, you may need to rebind the stems to make the dried bunch secure.

1 Take the spray of pink roses as your starting point. Add a 'collar' of mint at an approximate angle of 45° around the flowers. Next add 'collars' of valerian, sage and so on until you have used up all of your stems of flowers and foliage, finishing the posy with an edging of lady's mantle and finally ivy leaves. Turn the tussie mussie every so often to make sure that you are keeping a symmetrical shape and that your materials are at the right height to give you a smoothly rounded shape.

2 Bind the tussie mussie firmly with floral tape, though not so tightly that the flowers and herbs become crushed together. Cut the stems level and make sure that there are no sharp ends of thorns left on the part that will be held.

Lay the tussie mussie on a table and tie the two ribbons around the stems to finish it off.

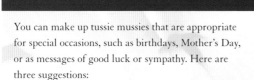

You can make up tussie mussies that are appropriate for special occasions, such as birthdays, Mother's Day, or as messages of good luck or sympathy. Here are three suggestions:

HERBAL OR PHYSIC
lady's mantle (protection), eucalyptus (get well), lavender (luck), pinks (love). Some of these flowers also have antiseptic ingredients

WINTER
hellebore (ward off evil powers), myrtle (love), ivy (friendship/fidelity), fir (time), rosemary (remembrance)

WINTER

A LOVE TOKEN
rosemary (remembrance), garden daisy (innocence), geum, red spray rose (bashful love), lavender (luck), cornflower (loyalty), honeysuckle, (lasting pleasure, generous affection or devotion)

HERBAL OR PHYSIC

A LOVE TOKEN

Pot pourri

FLOWERS AND MATERIALS

6 cups of highly scented rose petals
1 cup bay leaves
1 tbsp crushed orange peel
1 tbsp ground mace
1 crushed cinnamon stick
1 tbsp crushed cloves
2 tbsp crushed allspice
½ cup orris root
1 crushed star anise
2 cups of coarse salt *(non-iodized)*
pestle and mortar
an airtight container

THE ELIZABETHANS would, in fact, have been puzzled by this title, for the term pot pourri was not in general use until the mid-eighteenth century. Literally translated, it means 'rotten pot' and was used originally as a culinary term, but came to define a scented mix of petals. As rose petals were usually the main ingredient in early recipes an alternative name was rose bowl, although it is likely that any scented materials to hand would have been put to good use.

Traditional pot pourri usually contained scented petals or flower heads, wood, roots or bark, herbs, spices and fixatives. The fixative is what binds the aromatic elements together, intensifies the scent and makes it last. Orris root is a traditional fixative, made from the dried and powdered root of the Florentine iris with its own subtle violet scent. It is commonly available from health food shops and chemists, and can be bought in small quantities. There are two basic methods for making pot pourri – moist and dry. The moist method takes more effort, but reaps huge rewards as the fragrance is far more powerful and long lasting.

Moist Pot Pourri

This form is not usually displayed in an open container because of its unattractive appearance. Instead it is kept in a bowl or box with a pierced fretwork lid to allow the scent to escape. If you want to display your moist pot pourri in an open bowl, 'dress' the surface with dried roses and pretty single flower heads..

To make the base mixture, take some highly scented rose petals and lay them on newspaper to dry out for a couple of days. Take a storage jar and put a layer of approximately 1cm/ ½ inch of rose petals into the bottom of the jar, then sprinkle with the salt. Repeat this process until the jar is full, finishing off with a layer of salt.

Work on the proportions of three parts of petals to one of salt in each layer.

Stand your jar in a warm, dark place for about two weeks or until you can see that the petals are beginning to cake together. Don't be alarmed if your mixture starts to froth, just stir it every day and leave for a further two weeks.

2 Crumble the caked petals into a basin along with the dried herbs, spices and orris root that you have crushed in a pestle and mortar. Give the mixture a good stir until all the elements are thoroughly distributed.

Place the pot pourri mixture in an airtight container for a further five weeks to ferment. It is now ready to be transferred into a pierced lidded bowl. After all the hard work, you should find this deliciously scented pot pourri will last for years.

Dry Pot Pourri

This produces a pretty mixture that is ideal for displaying in a basket or bowl. You may find that the scent fades after a while, so will need to be topped up with a few drops of essential oils every six months or so.

FLOWERS AND MATERIALS

1 cup blue delphiniums
4 cups rose petals
1 cup rose buds
2 cups lavender flowers
2 cups lemon verbena
2 cups bay leaves
2 cups bergamot
1 cup angelica leaves
25g/1oz orris root
½ tsp ground cloves
2 drops sandalwood oil
2 drops rose oil
2 drops rosemary oil
2 mixing bowls
wooden spoon
airtight container

1 Mix together the orris root and ground spices in a non-metallic bowl (metal bowls and spoons could taint the oils). Add the essential oils. The materials need to be thoroughly mixed together, so you may need to wear gloves to protect your hands from the essential oils if not using a spoon.

To dress the top of the bowl, set aside some pretty flower heads and botanicals to avoid damaging them in the mixing process. In a separate bowl, mix all your 'dry' materials together, then add the mixture of crushed spices and fixatives. Thoroughly mix all the materials together to make sure that the scent blends through the pot pourri.

2 Put the mixture in an airtight container and leave in a warm, dark place for about five weeks. Shake the container every so often, especially during the first two weeks. The longer the mixture is stored in this container, the more potent the pot pourri will eventually be.

Tip the pot pourri into a pretty bowl or basket, top dressing it with the flowers and botanicals put aside earlier.

Orange and clove pomander

FLOWERS AND MATERIALS

an orange *(non-juicy fruit are best so try
    Seville oranges, or you can use a lemon
    or large lime)*
small tsp ground cinnamon and ground
    nutmeg *(optional)*
approx 50g (2oz) cloves
a generous tsp powdered orris root
1 metre *(1 yard)* velvet ribbon
1 metre *(1 yard)* narrow satin ribbon
masking tape
paperbag or tissue paper
a knitting needle or wooden skewer
scissors
glue
pins

POMANDER is derived from *pomme d'ambre*, apple of amber, and in its earliest form was in use in the thirteenth century. Similar varieties to this orange and clove pomander were very much a feature of the early sixteenth century. Spiced pomanders, like tussie mussies, were thought to have the power to ward off diseases including the plague. Along with strewing herbs, pot pourri and tussie mussies, they were also useful in disguising the unpleasant smells that were part of an everyday life without the benefits of modern sanitation and personal hygiene.

The intoxicating scent of this traditional pomander will last for years and is well worth the small amount of effort taken to assemble it. Cloves are a natural preservative and they are the ingredient that will 'cure' your orange. The powdered orris root (see p.24) will act as a fixative to bind together the scents and to make them last longer. Make your pomanders at least five weeks before you want to start using them to allow time for them to dry out properly.

For a hand-held pomander rather than one that hangs from the ribbons, adopt the same method as above, but in step 1 push a cinnamon stick firmly into the orange to act as a handle, and omit step 2.

You should find that your pomander's scent lasts for at least five or six years, and you can add a few drops of orange, cinnamon or clove oil to refresh it after this.

For a winter decoration you could make pomanders using different sizes of oranges, lemons or limes and omitting the hanging loops. Display them in a bowl or basket along with some large pine cones. Grapefruits, which are usually too heavy to hang up, can also be displayed in a bowl.

1 Pin a piece of masking tape around the middle of the orange, adding another to dissect this to mark out the four quarters. You are masking off the area that will eventually hold the ribbons, so cut the masking tape slightly wider than the width of the ribbons.

Working on one segment of the orange at a time, make small holes with the knitting needle or wooden skewer all over the non-masked areas of the orange. Leave a gap of about 0.5cm (¼in) between each hole, as your orange will shrink considerably as it dries. Firmly push a clove into each hole.

Remove the masking tape from the orange which is now covered in cloves. Mix together in the paper bag the ground orris root and powdered spice. Put the orange into the bag and shake gently until you feel that the whole surface has been thoroughly covered

with the mixture. Remove the spice-covered orange and wrap in tissue paper or another paper bag, and put in the airing cupboard (or an equivalent warm and dry place) for at least three to five weeks. Turn your orange every few days to help it to dry evenly and prevent the juice from pooling, which could result in rotting.

You can re-use your powdered spice mixture to cure more pomanders or recycle it into a batch of winter pot pourri (see p. 24-5). If you are making a large number of pomanders, you may find it easier to mix the powdered orris root and spice mixture in a large bowl, adding the fruit one by one and using a spoon to 'pour' the mixture over the oranges as you turn them. When you think they are thoroughly covered with the mixture, put each one into a separate paper bag or piece of tissue before storing in the airing cupboard.

2 Remove the orange and brush off any excess mixture from the surface. Now it's time to add your ribbons so that the pomander can be hung up. Had you added them earlier, you would have risked spoiling the fabric with the spice mixture.

Tie or glue a piece of ribbon around the middle of the orange where there are no cloves. Repeat in the other direction, making a hanging loop at the top.

FLOWERS AND MATERIALS

dried rosebuds in your choice of colour
1 metre (1 yard) of ribbon
a ball of florist's foam (I've used a
    tennis ball size)
scissors
stub wires
pva glue (optional) in a saucer

STREWING HERBS

These fulfilled many purposes: they masked pungent odours, soaked up debris and were more pleasant than walking on damp, cold and musty floors.

Strewing in its simplest form consisted of laying dried heather or straw on the floor, especially in kitchen areas to soak up debris. A new clean layer would subsequently be added until it reached the top of the threshold, when the whole lot was taken out and the process begun again. This gave rise to the saying 'going over the threshold'.

Herbs such as elacampane, sweet flag, bay, mint and lavender were commonly used for strewing.

Dried rosebud pomander

This type of pomander owes more to the romantic Victorian style, but is a pretty way to scent wardrobes or rooms (try hanging one on the curtain pole so that the perfume is wafted around the room when you draw the curtains). You will use a slightly different method to that for orange and clove pomanders, and may need to re-scent your pomander every six months or so.

Grade your rosebuds so that you use buds which are a consistent size and not too open.

Push a piece of stub wire through the centre of the ball of florist's foam and form a small hook at one end. Tie a small piece of ribbon onto this hook, then take up the slack on the wire so that the ribbon and hook are tight against the ball (the purpose of this piece of ribbon and hook is to stop the wire from pulling back through the foam). Cut off the stub wire leaving just enough protruding out of the foam to make a hook at this end. Before you push the end of the hook into the foam ball, pull your long piece of ribbon through the hook. Tie the ends of ribbon together and pull the knotted end down until the knot touches the foam ball. It will then appear that you have used a continuous piece of ribbon for your hanging loop.

Firmly push the hard stem end of the rosebuds into your ball. If you want to make absolutely sure that they cannot fall out, dip the end of the stem into pva glue before pushing into the foam. Position each bud next to the previous one so that you do not see any of the foam beneath. This is why it is useful to grade the rosebuds before you start, to ensure a neat and symmetrical arrangement. Continue until all the foam is covered. If you have a tiny gap, just glue in a very small bud.

TIPS

To re-scent this pomander, add a few drops of rose oil once or twice a year. Hang it out of direct sunlight to prevent premature fading. Yellow rosebuds seem to fade more quickly than other colours.

If you are storing your dried rosebuds for any length of time, remember to seal them in an airtight container. Moths will quickly eat their way through your supply if they can get through the smallest hole in a plastic bag.

Other suggestions for pomanders include clove and cardamom, rose and cardamom, statice, star anise and clove, and pot pourri. For a pot pourri pomander, prepare your ball of floral foam with wire and ribbon, then brush pva glue over the ball before rolling it in fine-grade pot pourri. Allow the glue to dry, then glue on individual flowers to cover any holes and to add focal interest.

Stuart ingenuity

The Stuarts loved rich colours, and these can
be seen in the selection of flowers that I have
made to encapsulate the seventeenth century.
Some are what we would consider as wild
flowers – buttercups, daisies, honeysuckle,
lady's mantle, cow parsley, periwinkle, mallow
and valerian. Others were cultivated in gardens
– roses, the longiflorum lily, marigolds, pinks,
sweet Williams, lavender and geums. Much
prized by the Stuarts were exotic introductions,
such as the tulip, which reached England from
Turkey *c*. 1578, and the sunflower from North
America. The great painter Anthony van Dyck
chose to depict himself with a sunflower in his
self-portrait.

STUART INGENUITY

The Stuarts, who reigned from 1603 to 1714, wrought havoc with civil war, but they also brought Britain into much closer contact with Europe and the rest of the world through their family ties with France, Italy and Holland. Although this was not regarded by all their subjects as a good thing, from the artistic and cultural points of view, Britain was immeasurably richer as a result.

Ham House, on the banks of the Thames near Richmond, provides an excellent example of seventeenth-century style. The interior reflects the style of two periods: first, the 1630s when the Earl of Dysart furnished several of the rooms; and secondly of the 1670s when his daughter Elizabeth, Duchess of Lauderdale created one of the most lavishly appointed houses of the day. The North Drawing Room shows the influence of French court style of the earlier period, with a rich marble chimneyiece flanked by twisted columns decorated in gilt. The Lauderdales were leading members of the Charles II's court, and when they laid out their private rooms on the ground floor, they reflected the very formal style of life of the King's cousin, Louis XIV of France, with rooms leading away from the public Marble Dining Room into their separate apartments consisting of withdrawing room, bedchamber, dressing room and, most private of all, the closet.

Inventories made at the end of the seventeenth century give details of the colours and fabrics used as furnishings at Ham. Like the Elizabethans, the Stuarts revelled in rich, bold colours. The Duchess Elizabeth chose yellow and blue for her bedchamber, and purple and gold for her private closet. These colours are also reflected in the fashionable dress of the period: portraits of Charles II's courtiers shows the sitters in shimmering silk dresses of gold, russet and yellow. When the diarist Samuel Pepys sat for his portrait, he chose a rich golden brown silk 'nightgown' (informal dress). He described this gown as Indian although in form it looks more like a Japanese kimono. His geography may have been vague, but his interest in the new and exciting goods coming from the East was intense.

above: Detail of the North Drawing Room at Ham House, Surrey, showing one of the of the flamboyant twisted columns that flank the chimneypiece.

Exoticism and ingenuity were qualities much admired in the seventeenth century. When Mary Stuart came to England with her Dutch consort, William III, in 1688, she was also accompanied by shrubs known as exotics – plants from abroad – and greens – evergreens. Tender varieties were over-wintered in orangeries, greenhouses and hothouses equipped with stoves. Special wheeled vehicles were created to move large plants such as orange and lemon trees so that they could be brought into the garden in summer. Boxes were designed to allow volumes of cut flowers to be transported in winter, wrapped in moss bindings to prolong their lives.

Queen Mary also brought her great collection of blue and white porcelain from China and Japan, which was displayed in a special gallery at Hampton Court. The taste for oriental china was taken up by her courtiers.

right: The Duke of Lauderdale's closet at Ham House, where the hangings were of black and olive-coloured damask trimmed with scarlet. Some of the Lauderdales' collection of blue and white porcelain can be seen on the right.

For those with less money at their disposal, blue and white delftware was available not only from Holland but also from English factories: I have described some of the styles of containers for plants and flowers on pp.38-9.

Dutch flower paintings of the period provide an excellent reference for the kinds of flowers used in arrangements and the style in which they were arranged. One of the great seventeenth-century favourites was the tulip. This had been introduced from Turkey into western Europe c.1578. but the craze for the plants really took off in the 1630s in Holland, with fortunes won and lost on a single bulb. Striped tulips were particularly sought after, and the desire for the unusual applied to other flowers too – speckles, spots of contrasting colour, double forms on carnations, pinks, narcissi and auriculas, for example.

We have to use these flower paintings with caution, however. The varieties of flowers cross the seasons, and the angles at which they are arranged indicate that the blooms could not have had their cut stems in water. These pictures were often commissioned by wealthy

above: Swags of fruit and flowers carved by the ingenious seventeenth-century craftsman, Edward Pierce, in the Saloon at Sudbury Hall, Derbyshire.

patrons to show off the highly-prized, new varieties of plants to be found in their gardens. For some the plants were so prohibitively expensive that the painting was the one way to enjoy a lasting image. However, they do provide clues to the form of arrangements.

In the early seventeenth century these tended to be round or oval in shape, tightly packed with flowers with a solid outline to the display, but with no prominent focal point. Flowers of all colours were mixed together, usually containing at least a couple of red blooms. By the middle of the century a looser form was developed with flowers pointing in all directions, even at the back of the arrangement. This looseness continued through to the end of the century, with a sweeping 's' shape emerging. Large-headed flowers like the sunflower, and exotic fruit such as the pineapple were introduced to provide a dramatic top to the arrangement.

Dyrham Park, just outside Bristol, provides a good

example of the style of house in fashion at the very end of the Stuart period. Its creator, William Blathwayt, was Secretary at War to William III, and spent much of his time in Holland. He was also Commissioner for the Colonies, and thus able to import exotics from the New World. The Best Staircase at Dyrham was constructed from American cedar, while the walls were painted a rich

above: The Best Staircase at Dyrham Park, Gloucestershire, showing the golden marbling on the walls, and vases and sweetmeat dishes from William Blathwayt's collection of delftware from Holland.

gold yellow which was then ingeniously marbled. This provides a fine backdrop to some of the blue and white delftware from Blathwayt's collection.

Stuart containers

BOUGH (bow) pots continued to be fashionable in the seventeenth century. They were often very large and used to display flowers and foliage in fireplaces where they were less likely to be knocked over. Containers of all sizes often had pierced lids to support the stems.

By the end of the century, blue and white ware had become extremely fashionable. Queen Mary had brought over from Holland her collection of oriental porcelain and tin-glazed earthenware from Delft, and this set the trend.

Perhaps the most spectacular of the containers were flower pyramids, which are sometimes known as tulip vases. In fact, they could be used for the display of a variety of flowers. Another exotic shape was the five-fingered quintal horn – the earliest known example of this type was found in Mary's garden room at her Dutch palace, Het Loo. Flower bricks in blue and white were also introduced at this time.

Blue and white vase

above: A delftware flower brick with scabious, jasmine, pink veronica, cistus, pansies, lady's mantle, pinks, rose and cornflower.

Quintal horn (finger vase)

Silver ewer

38

Plaster candlestick

Gilded urn

Bough pot with pierced lid

Hyacinth
vase

Blue and white cache pot

Flower bricks

Upright urn arrangement

FLOWERS AND MATERIALS

2 stems sunflower
marigolds
larkspur
feverfew
yarrow
celosia
lady's mantle
peonies
convulvulus
corn cockles
cornflowers
antirrhinum
zinnia
red spray roses
meadowsweet
ivy
tobacco plants
3 blocks wet floral foam
floral tape
secateurs
scissors
blue and white pot

SEVENTEENTH-CENTURY flower arrangements combined a variety of colours rather than matching the particular colour scheme of a room. Virtually no foliage was used, save that actually found on the stems of the flowers themselves. The flowers were not crowded together, nor did they have a central focal area as seen in modern decorations. A natural balance of symmetry was sought, with some of the large-headed flowers at the top of the arrangement. Flower stems were added in an upright fashion, with the heads of the blooms facing in all directions.

These arrangements were made in vases and urn-shaped pots with two handles, often rather confusingly referred to as pots or flower pots. With little furniture kept in the centre of a room, these vases were often displayed on brackets, pediments above doors, window ledges, occasional side tables, and fireplaces during the summer months. The Elizabethan fashion for bough pots, vases of sufficient capacity to hold quite large branches of flowers and foliage, still thrived. These were usually displayed in the fireplace where there was less risk of being knocked over.

Thoroughly soak the floral foam. Tape the blocks firmly into position. Start by arranging some of the longest flower stems to give an overall outline of the arrangement – the celosia, spray roses, feverfew, marigolds, larkspur, and tendrils of ivy. These stems should be added in an upright position as though they are self supporting within the container. Remember to vary the angle and directions of the stems as you work.

2 Infill the gaps between the main flowers, trying to ensure that each bloom can be seen individually and not crushed together.

TIPS

As Stuart households would use quantities of wild 'field flowers' to infill their focal flowers, you may decide against using floral foam, which does not always suit wild flowers. An alternative way to make this arrangement would be to insert some chicken wire into the container and then fill it at least half full with water. If you are using plain galvanised wire, you may want to line your container with a separate plastic bowl to prevent scratching. This wire framework will

allow you to position the stems securely and easily top up the container with water. Regularly replace any fading flowers.

When selecting your sunflowers, remember that the cut stem ends often harden off if they are out of water too long because of their fibrous nature. To encourage the stems to draw water effectively, recut the ends and give them a drink of warm water for an hour before conditioning them in tepid water.

Garlanding

FLOWERS AND MATERIALS

roses
love-in-a-mist
cow parsley
honeysuckle
lavender
foliage of ivy, rosemary, bay
    and myrtle
moss (this is optional, but will
    make a thicker garland, and help
    to make it last longer) or hay
serrated scissors
reel wire or string
thin rope

THE TERM 'GARLAND' seems to have come into general use during the Middle Ages, but the custom of twining foliage and flowers together is very ancient.

Garlands could be made throughout the year with any seasonal foliage, and with large numbers of flowers for high status celebrations. During the seventeenth century these were a very popular form of decoration, often used in profusion draped on and around the buffet, where the household's plate was displayed.

1 Before starting to work, ensure that the ends of the piece of rope are singed to prevent unravelling. Make a secure hanging loop at either end using the reel wire. Bind generous handfuls of damp moss or hay onto the rope base, using the reel of wire or string.

2 Make small bunches with the foliage and flowers, binding each bunch individually with a piece of reel wire. This will allow you to lay the bunches along the rope to see how many more to make, and enables you to alter the placement of the bunches to give a good, even thickness.

3 Start wiring the bunches onto the mossed rope with the head of the first covering the hanging loop at one end of the garland. Hold the stems of the first bunch onto the base and catch the reel wire around this several times before creating a 'blanket stitch' by making a wide loop with the wire and then passing the whole reel through the loop and pulling firmly to take up any slack.

4 Continue adding the bunches to the base, ensuring that each bunch covers the stems of the previous one. When you reach the end of the garland, add a slightly more generous bunch to the base with the same method, but turn it in the opposite direction so that the head now covers the remaining loop. Make several 'blanket stitches', cut the wire and feed the sharp cut end into the moss.

TIPS

Always measure the area to be decorated with the rope that you are planning on using. A flat tape measure can often give an unrealistic measurement because it hangs differently.

The amount of time that you want your garland to last will dictate the most appropriate method of making it up. If you are making a thick garland as a Christmas decoration and want it to last for over a week, you may want to use a base of chicken wire and wet floral foam (see p.65). If you are making a summer-time celebration garland, you could use a moss and rope base, putting it together the day before it is needed and leaving in a cool place overnight. A garland of hardy foliage should last outdoors for at least a week or two using the bin

bag base, or the combination of chicken wire and wet floral foam.

If you are planning to drape your garland Stuart style around serving dishes and plates, do remember that many flowers and foliage are highly toxic (for example, ivy, yew, aconitum, foxglove, lily of the valley, holly berries). Therefore keep well away from food in case an unlucky guest ends up nibbling part of your decoration!

To hang your garland on textiles such as a tablecloth, pin securely using pearl-headed pins so that the loops cannot slip.

To maintain the garland, especially if made on a dry base of bin bags or ribbon, mist spray regularly or move to a cooler situation every evening. Protect the paint- or woodwork or

textiles when misting with water by sliding a large piece of cardboard between the surface and the garland. Put a towel beneath the garland for a couple of hours to catch any drips. You may decide to 'water' the garland at night and remove the towel in the morning.

ALTERNATIVE METHODS FOR MAKING THE GARLAND

a) Follow steps 1 and 2 but make your individual bunches up by catching the stems together with a length of stub wire, leaving a generous amount of wire at the end of each bunch. To attach these bunches to your base, push the end of the stub wire through the moss until it comes out at the back. Firmly wrap the end of the wire around the mossed or hay base.

b) Follow method **(a)** but choosing from a variety of different materials as the base. These include wide ribbon or a bin bag (cut down both sides to form a long rectangle and then rolled to form a plastic 'rope'). You can also use small rectangles of wet floral foam wrapped in cling film and twisted between each block of foam to create a string of 'foam sausages'. If you are using soft-stemmed flowers for this,

you may want to use a wooden skewer to pierce holes in the cling film before adding the materials.

Another method is to take a length of chicken wire wrapped around the wet floral foam to make a sausage roll shape (see p.65). But beware with all of these methods that the bases could stretch if too many heavy materials are used.

In this close-up of another garland, I have used daisies, nasturtiums, love-in-a-mist, marigolds, lavender, pansies, cornflowers, roses and scabious with foliage of ivy, myrtle, rosemary, bay and box.

Table decorations

FLOWERS AND MATERIALS

2 stems eryngium thistles
9 stems statice
5 stems jasmine
3 stems golden rod
6 stems lady's mantle
5 stems yarrow
3 stems asters
9 stems sweet Williams
3 stems passion flowers
12 stems anemones
3 stems marigolds
10 stems pinks
10 stems cornflowers
3 blocks of wet floral foam in
   a waterproof bowl
a large footed pot
floral tape or chicken wire
scissors
secateurs

DURING THE SEVENTEENTH CENTURY, dinner was the main meal of the day, taken in late morning. It usually consisted of two courses and almost certainly there was no form of flower arrangement on the table during these because of the sheer quantity of plates of meat, fish, and pies. There are, however, descriptions of the room itself being decorated with flower-filled bowls, jugs, vases and garlands.

Sometimes a third course would be served, known as the banquet. Later in the century, this course began to be referred to as the dessert, from the French *desservir*, to clear the table. It was often taken in a separate withdrawing room, or in grand households in a completely separate building, the banqueting house, in the garden.

The banqueting house would be decked with garlands and boughs of flowers and foliage, and with strewing herbs and rushes on the floor. An upright, central flower arrangement could be set up in the centre of the table, on a shaped wooden or wicker board, an early version of the eighteenth-century *surtout de table*. This would be surrounded by pyramids of fresh and preserved fruits trimmed with flowers (often themselves preserved with sugar and water). Around the edge of these would sit the plates of sweetmeats, biscuits and sugar paste flowers within easy reach of guests.

The buffet displaying the household plate could also be decorated with a profusion of swags of flowers and foliage (see pp.42-5), together with more tiered pyramids of fruit and flowers.

I Thoroughly soak the floral foam, tape securely into the container and position inside the pot. Set the shape and height of your arrangement using a stem of eryngium thistles with statice at mid-level and short stems of jasmine around the lip of the container.

2 Add some golden rod, lady's mantle and yarrow to form a softly curving line between the flowers at the base of the foam and those at the top of the arrangement, thus setting the overall width. Remember to keep turning the pot so that you can view it from all sides, as it will be seen when completed and in position on the table.

3 Infill the gaps between the large flowers, trying to ensure that each bloom can be seen individually and not crushed together. Top up your container with water, as the flowers will draw the greatest amount in the first twenty-four hours that they are in the foam.

TIPS

As this arrangement uses quantities of short-stemmed flowers, you may decide against using floral foam as it does not always suit some flowers such as anemones. Instead, you can insert chicken wire into the container to act as a support for the stems and then fill it at least half full with water. If you are using plain galvanised wire, you may want to line your container with a separate plastic bowl to prevent scratching.

This wire framework will allow you to position the stems securely, and more easily to top up with water regularly and replace any fading flowers.

When using floral foam for this type of arrangement, ensure that it is slightly lower than the top edge of the container, so that the stems can cover the edge rather than look as though they are hanging down over it.

Georgian
elegance

The Georgians loved flowers that were
delicate both in form and in colour, and in
their arrangements sought to enhance the
individual shape of each bloom. These
qualities have influenced the flowers that
I have chosen to represent the eighteenth
century. Delicacy is represented by
buttercups, cornflowers, daisies, lady's
mantle, lavender, mallows, geums, pansies,
sweet peas, scabious, cranesbill, feverfew,
and valerian. For their garlands, Georgians
often used roses, peonies and honeysuckle
with mixed foliage.

GEORGIAN ELEGANCE

The predominant influence on eighteenth-century style was the classical. Upper-class Englishmen had travelled in Europe to complete their education in the previous century, but the Grand Tour – principally of Italy, Switzerland and the Netherlands – really took off in the early 1700s. English milords returned with works of art, ideas on architecture, landscape gardening and, later in the century, interest in archaeology.

The end of Elizabeth I's reign coincided conveniently with the beginning of the seventeenth century, the Stuart dynasty came to an end as far as the English throne was concerned with the death of Queen Anne in 1714. The Hanoverians were not quite so neat: the first four Georges reigned right through to 1830, and William IV until 1837. For the purposes of this book, we are treating the eighteenth century as the Georgian age.

This period saw a range of styles, from the strict rules of Palladianism to the frivolous and ornate Rococo, Gothick Revival and Chinoiserie, back to the austere neo-classicism and the archaeological interpretations of Pompeian and Etruscan. There are more eighteenth-century country houses in Britain open to the public than from any other period, so the various styles can easily be seen. Clandon Park in Surrey, designed by the Venetian architect Giacomo Leoni in the 1730s is a good example of restrained Palladianism, in strong contrast to the exuberant Rococo interior of Claydon House in Buckinghamshire where Luke Lightfoot produced fantastic wood-carving. Claydon also has some wonderful Chinoiserie decoration, while Nostell Priory in Yorkshire contains fine furniture in the oriental style by Thomas Chippendale. Berrington Hall in Herefordshire, designed in the neo-classical style by Henry Holland c.1780, shows

above: Detail of the Marble Hall at Clandon Park, Surrey with 'bough pots' on the hearth and a classical relief dedication to Bacchus, the Greek god of wine, in the overmantel.

the return to restraint by the neo-classicists. Ickworth in Suffolk has a Pompeian Room, and Osterley Park in Middlesex an Etruscan Dressing Room.

It is therefore difficult to sum up Georgian style, but the overriding factor was that the classical Roman ideals in architecture and decoration were considered by eighteenth-century architects and their patrons to be elegance and calm solemnity. This was a period of unprecedented expansion for Britain, with colonies established in North America, India and Australasia, and supremacy on the high seas bringing great wealth to Britain – or rather, to those with power and privilege.

One such was the banker Francis Child, who commissioned Robert Adam to remodel the Tudor house at Osterley. Adam designed the Etruscan Dressing Room in 1772, basing his scheme on the black and terracotta colours he had seen on antique vases and on reproductions being made by Josiah Wedgwood. He set them on a sky-blue background to give the effect of being out of doors. The fashionable colours of the later eighteenth century were pale and very varied. Adam considered specific colours as being appropriate for certain rooms: stone for halls, red for morning rooms and picture galleries, green for bedrooms, and so on.

One visitor to the Etruscan Dressing Room at Osterley remarked that it was 'painted all over like Wedgwood's ware ... . It is like going out of a palace into a potter's field.' However, this was not the time to sneer at potters. Wedgwood's influence on the lifestyle of the period was enormous. The Georgians loved what

right: The exotic Rococo woodwork in the North Hall of Claydon House in Buckinghamshire.

above: A detail from the Marble Hall at Berrington in Herefordshire, showing a trophy of arms surrounded by a classical garland.

they called 'glister'. Pale colours, mirrors, gilded furniture and the softly gleaming surfaces of porcelain could all enhance the light from candlelabra and chandeliers.

Flowers were an integral part of decoration. Ladies wore them in their elaborately dressed hair, carried posies, bouquets or baskets, and pinned corsages to their gowns. The overall style of arranging flowers was natural and even haphazard. Many different varieties were combined, usually with their own natural foliage. Multiple stems of flowers were used, but rather than being crushed together, they were placed so that each bloom could be admired in its own right. A delicate palette of pastel shades was preferred to dramatic contrasts.

Garlands, with their classical connotations, were one of the must-have decorations for fashionable homes throughout Europe. They could be made of fresh or artificial flowers or foliage, or even feathers, to drape over statues, columns, pictures, side tables and dining tables to create an air of elegant formality for balls, routs or intimate parties.

right: Robert Adam's Etruscan Dressing Room at Osterley Park, Middlesex.

Georgian containers

THE DEVELOPMENT of first hard paste, then soft
paste porcelain in European factories such as Meissen and
Sèvres led to a wonderful variety of containers for flowers
and plants. Basket shapes could be produced not only in
wicker, but metal and soft paste porcelain too.

Josiah Wedgwood founded his pottery at Burslem in
Staffordshire in 1759 and began to produce earthenware in
simple, elegant patterns that appealed to customers with a
taste for neo-classicism. He continued to make traditional
containers such as bough pots, vases with pierced lids and
quintals, but also developed a new idea, wall pockets or
cornucopia, which he also called faces and flower horns.
From 1774 he produced his famous Jasperware with relief
decorations on blue, lavender, green or yellow ground,
based on the shapes and decorations of Greek vases.

left: Urn with flat-backed arrangement
(see p.69).

Painted wooden cache pot

*Quintal horn
(finger vase)*

*Selection of
Wedgwood
Jasperware*

Silver ewer

Wall pocket vase

Porcelain urn

Tiered stand

Basket

Bough pot with pierced lid

Bulb pot

Porcelain vase

Flower brick

Posies

GEORGIAN POSIES or nosegays were often used to carry a message from the sender to the recipient through the choice of flowers and foliage. This practice was continued and developed into a complex and subtle language by the Victorians.

Eighteenth-century posies were usually informal and, although perfumed flowers and foliage were often included, they were by no means as fundamental as they would have been to Elizabethan tussie mussies.

The combination of flowers and foliage used here could be interpreted as 'I was reminded of your loveliness and innocence at our unexpected meeting. I am perplexed by our painful but pleasurable love. You are in my thoughts. I shall remain silent and protect your virtue always.' Nevertheless, the potential for misinterpreting such messages is alarming, for many flowers appear to have had numerous and often conflicting symbolism.

I Hold a selection of the stems of the flowers and foliage in one hand so that the heads are relatively level and the stems roughly parallel. If this is the first time you have made a hand-tied posy, you may find it useful to bind the stems of the bunch together every so often so that you don't grip the stems too tightly. To do this, stick the end of the floral tape onto the mid-point of the stems and wind it around the forming bunch.

2 Continue adding flowers and foliage around the bunch in a random fashion so that the flowers are evenly distributed throughout the posy. Tilt its 'head' every so often so that you can gauge the overall shape and density as you wrap it with the tape.

As you are nearing the outside edge of the posy, stagger the flowers slightly down so that they cover the bare stems of the earlier flowers. When you have used all the stems, bind the posy one last time with floral tape and then tie your ribbon over this.

TIPS

Your posy should stay fresh for up to a week if left in water. If you are making it for a gift or special occasion, you can easily arrange it the day before, putting it in a glass of water. Do not add the ribbon at this stage. Remove the posy from the water at least an hour before you need it, dry the base of the stems with a

towel, tie on the ribbons and then stand the bunch upright in a dry glass. If you leave it resting on one side for too long, you will end up with a flattened edge.

These posies are surprisingly easy to dry. Hang them upside down in a well-ventilated place that is out of direct sunlight to prevent bleaching

out the colour before the flowers and foliage have actually dried. In the summer you may well be able to dry the posy in two weeks. As the flowers and foliage will shrink slightly as they dry, you may need to rebind the stems to make the bunch secure.

Basketware arrangement

FLOWERS AND MATERIALS

honeysuckle
sweet peas
lady's mantle
roses
love-in-a-mist
campanula
daisies
mallow
cow parsley
cornflowers
gypsophila
delphiniums or larkspur
Brompton stocks
spray roses
scabious
alliums
jasmine
gentians
a basket with plastic inner
    container
floral foam
stub wires
wire cutters
secateurs
scissors

FOR MOST OF THE EIGHTEENTH CENTURY, furniture was positioned along the walls of rooms when not in use. Flower tables were made as individual pieces or in sets of three slotted into each other, called quartetti. These would stand in window embrasures to take vases of flowers.

By the later part of the century the fashion for exuberant – and expensive – Rococo-style porcelain was on the decline. Instead, the trend was for more classical, restrained elegance, which was quickly exploited by Josiah Wedgwood with his range of soft paste creamware and the severely neo-classical Jasperware in various colours.

The fashion in flower arrangements was to adopt an irregular shape which gave a natural rather than contrived appearance. In keeping with this, the containers took on the form of baskets – either in wire or metal, or in soft paste porcelain.

These baskets could decorate not only flower tables but also mantelpieces and containers attached to pier glasses.

Cut the floral foam to fit the basket and push into the waterproof container. Bend some stub wires into hairpin shapes and slot them through the weave of the basket.

2 Set the shape of the arrangement by using three tall flowers at the back of the foam, positioning them asymmetrically. Randomly add other stems of flowers at the front of the container so that they hang slightly over the lip of the basket.

3 Infill the gaps between the flowers, trying to ensure that each bloom looks as if it has been placed spontaneously and can be seen individually. Regularly top up the container with water.

TIPS

If you are using wild flowers, you may decide against using floral foam, which does not always suit them. An alternative is to insert some chicken wire into the container and then fill it at least half full with water. The wire framework will allow you to position the stems securely and easily top up the container with water. Regularly replace any fading flowers.

Place hairpin stub wires well above the water line to avoid puncturing the plastic container, causing a leak.

59

Formal table arrangement

FLOWERS AND MATERIALS

For the garlanding:
10 stems of flowering jasmine, or
    10 stems soft ruscus
small-headed flowers
scissors
roll of stem wrap
green reel wire or string

For the baskets of flowers:
selection of flowers, including
    spray roses, feverfew, love-in-a-
    mist, cornflowers, larkspur buds,
    veronica, sweet peas, lady's
    mantle, sedum, antirrhinum,
    gypsophila
single leaves to line the basket
2 sizes of silver baskets
chicken wire
waterproof inner baskets

IN THE EIGHTEENTH CENTURY, the style of dining continued to be what we now call *à la française*, the main courses served as a series of dishes put on the table simultaneously. This left no space for decorations, so that, as in Stuart times, any flower arrangements were confined to the dessert course. The wooden or wicker board of the seventeenth century had given way to a central plateau called a *surtout de table,* made of mirror glass, porcelain or even silver. Onto this central plateau were placed numerous small vases or baskets of flowers, sometimes linked by delicate garlands. Fine strands of garlands could be held aloft by dancing nymph figurines made of porcelain or silver. As many as forty baskets of flowers and fruits could be used for special occasions.

By the 1740s these arrangements had become very elaborate, the flowers were sometimes fresh, sometimes made out of sugar paste so that they glittered in the candlelight. By the next decade porcelain was the material of choice for those who could afford it. Miniature landscapes including temples, cottages, trees, churches, and farms were set alongside huntsmen, fishermen, and farmers. This fashion was so widespread that shops offered not only to sell the porcelain figures but also hire them out to those who could not afford their own. Decorations in silver gilt, enamelled glass and cartonage (a form of gilded cardboard) were also available. This extravagant Rococo form of decoration gave way in the 1770s to a more severe, neo-classical style, with 'antique' urns in unglazed porcelain or marble. At this period too, the custom of bringing tables into the centre of the room for dining and then storing them against the wall or in the corridor outside was gradually replaced by having a long dining table permanently in position.

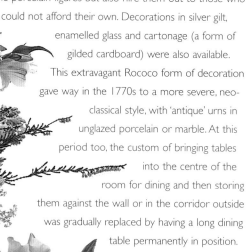

To make up the basket arrangements:

1 Bend the edges of the chicken wire down and put into the waterproof container to form a structure to support the stems.

2 Add some single large leaves between the two bowls to disguise the inner bowls through the pierced sides of the baskets. Set the shape of your arrangement by using the tallest central stem of antirrhinum in the middle of the chicken wire and then add a stem of flowers to sit against the edge of the basket at the far points. Start to add other stems at random, so that the chicken wire is no longer visible, but keeping the original shape.

Infill the gaps between the flowers, trying to ensure that each bloom looks spontaneously placed and can be seen individually. Regularly top up the container with water.

To make the garlanding:

Cut a length of reel wire or string to the size of the space to be garlanded. Wire can be useful here as it can be bent into specific shapes. Cut the jasmine or ruscus into small sections. Hold a section of jasmine onto the reel wire or string and bind it on holding the stem wrap against the stem and gently pulling the stem wrap with one hand whilst wrapping it around the stems and pinching it firmly. Stem wrap is not generally adhesive and reacts with the heat of your hands to make it stick to itself. By pulling gently the tape will stretch and become thinner, so that it bonds together easily.

Add the next piece of jasmine to cover the stem of the previous piece, and stem wrap. At regular intervals add a few small-headed flowers on top of a piece of jasmine foliage and continue in this way until you reach the end of the garland. Turn the last piece of jasmine in the opposite direction to cover the cut end of the wire or string, and stem wrap into position.

TIPS

Plastic-covered chicken wire is more expensive, but it is usually green and less sharp at the cut edges and therefore easier to work with. If you are using plain galvanised wire, you may want to line your basket or china container with a separate plastic bowl to make it waterproof and to prevent scratching.
By using chicken wire rather than floral foam, you can space the flowers well apart to achieve a

spontaneous feel without letting the workings of your arrangement be seen.
It also enables you to top up with water regularly and to replace any fading flowers.
If your hands are cold, you will find it difficult to get the stem wrap to adhere to itself. Put the tape somewhere warm before using it, then you will find it much easier to work with.

Garlanding

FLOWERS AND MATERIALS

auriculas
honeysuckle
sweet Williams
pink spray roses
peonies
passion flowers
box
ivy
bay
2 metres (2 yards) ribbon
wire ties or reel wire
serrated scissors
wet floral foam
a sharp knife
plastic-coated chicken wire

GARLANDS, OR WREATHS as they were often called, were very fashionable decorations throughout eighteenth-century Europe. In some households, garlands formed part of everyday decorations, rather than being reserved for special occasions.

Graceful early Georgian garlands and wreaths were influenced by the Rococo style. Less dramatic than their seventeenth-century predecessors, they would have been casually draped in an asymmetrical fashion. In the latter part of the eighteenth century, garlands became more delicate in design. Flower garlands were often swagged around the edges of tables, over pictures, statues, doors and window frames. Surprisingly, artificial flowers made from feathers, silk, silver, or sugar paste, were often preferred to fresh flowers, valued for their novelty and artifice.

During the early nineteenth century, table garlands could be incredibly fine, made with single stems of narrow pointed leaves interspersed with small clusters of tiny-headed flowers. These could be draped along the centre of the dining table to imitate its shape, held aloft by small figurines in porcelain or silver.

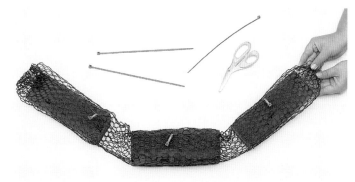

1 Soak the floral foam thoroughly, then cut the blocks down through the centre to make a pair of thick rectangles from each block. Cut the chicken wire to the required length and place the cut blocks of floral foam onto the centre of the wire, leaving a small gap between each block to allow you later to bend the garland frame to a swagged shape.

Wrap the edges of the chicken wire together to form a neat seam in the centre of the garland, firmly securing the edges together with wire ties, or 'stitching' down through the length of the wire using the reel wire. Fold the wire at either end of the base as if wrapping the ends of a parcel, and wire tie (or 'stitch') this into the chicken wire frame. Make a hanging loop of wire, or a wire tie at either end. Bend the base into the shape of the swag to fill the space to be decorated.

2 Starting at one end of the base, firmly push short stems of foliage through the chicken wire and into the floral foam (though not so forcefully that the cut stem ends go completely through the floral foam). The head of foliage should cover the hanging loop with the stem pointing towards the centre of the base. Repeat this at the other end. Work backwards into the centre of the base, adding stems of foliage as you go. Use slightly longer stems as you reach the middle of the base so that you have a fuller mid-section.

3 Now that the base contains a generous amount of foliage, you are ready to begin adding the focal flowers. Starting at either end, work towards the centre of the garland, using smaller flowers for the ends and positioning the largest flowers around the central area. You may decide to add a bow at either end of the garland – see p.11 for an easy way to make bows. See picture overleaf.

TIPS

Always measure the area to be decorated with the shape of the base you are planning to use. A flat tape measure can often give an unrealistic measurement because it will hang differently.

You may want to make your garland well in advance, so consider wrapping each block in cling film before you lay it onto the chicken wire. This will seal in the moisture and prevent any damage to wooden or painted surfaces on which the garland will hang. The drawback is that it is quite difficult to re-water the floral foam later as it is encased in the cling film.

To maintain the fresh flower garland, mist spray it regularly or move to a cooler place every evening. To protect paintwork, wood surfaces or textiles when misting, slide a large piece of cardboard recycled from a box between the surface and the garland. Use a long-spouted watering can carefully to trickle water into the centre of each block of floral foam, and place a towel beneath the garland for a couple of hours to catch any drips of water. You may decide to 'water' the garland at night so that you can remove the towel in the morning.

ALTERNATIVE METHODS

TWISTED GARLANDS
The simplest form of garlands is just a matter of entwining flowers and foliage. This can produce stunning garlands. Take two or three long stems of trailing ivy and hold the cut stem ends in one hand. Wire the stem ends together and make a hanging loop. Using your other hand, just flick one stem around the other two until you reach the tips, then wire these together and make another hanging loop.

These ivy bases can be submerged in water for several days until you are ready to decorate them with flowers. This will condition the ivy and wash off any unwanted mud or cobwebs. Simply add your flowers into this base by mounting each flower head on a piece of reel wire, positioning the flower in the ivy and then wrapping the reel wire around the base of the ivy stems.

This garland will be very flexible and can be used to decorate tables and the fronts of cloths. It can be twisted around columns, gates, or even bent in a complete circle to form a simple wreath shape.

OTHER GARLANDS
A variety of different materials can be used as a base, including a length of rope or wide ribbon, a bin bag (cut down both sides to form a long rectangle and rolled to form a plastic 'rope'), or willow or wicker frame (into which you tuck the stems of flowers and foliage). You can also use small rectangles of wet floral foam wrapped in cling film and twisted between each block of foam to create a string of 'foam sausages'. If you are using soft stemmed flowers for this, you may want to use a wooden skewer to pierce holes in the cling film before adding the materials. It is worth noting that, apart from the rope and wicker base methods, the bases could stretch if too many heavy materials are used.

Flat-backed urn arrangement

FLOWERS AND MATERIALS

3 stems pink spray roses
3 stems hebe
2 stems golden rod
6 stems cornflowers
5 stems honeysuckle
2 stems scabious
I stem celosia
3 stems alstroemeria
2 stems Brompton stocks
I white gladiolus
I stem September flowers
I stem lady's mantle
2 stems sedum
5 stems single asters
2 stems gypsophila
6 stems roses
2 stems white larkspur
a tall urn
2 blocks wet floral foam
plastic coated chicken wire
floral tape
a basket with a waterproof inner
scissors

THESE NEO-CLASSICAL urn-shaped vases were highly popular for side tables, mantelpieces and fireplaces. They were even placed underneath side tables, as the Georgians did not like empty spaces.

Revelling in the fashion for nature in all its glory, floral arrangements typically contained many varieties of flowers in one container. Extra foliage was not added.

These arrangement were loose and irregular, showing a natural balance rather than a forced symmetry and enabling the viewer to identify and appreciate each bloom in its own right. The earlier 'crowning glory' style was replaced with arrangements that contained large round flowers throughout.

These arrangements were often made in bough pots. In the eighteenth century manufacturers of these pots developed covered tops pierced with holes to enable the arranger to position the stems more easily, and to ensure that the flowers rose up out of the arrangement rather than hanging down too far over the lip of the container.

| Thoroughly soak the floral foam and securely tape it into the urn. Set the overall shape of the arrangement by positioning a tall stem of gladiolus at the back of the foam, just off the true centre. Add a curving stem of stock to the bottom right of the neck of the vase, and a stem of lady's mantle to the left-hand side to balance this.

*To avoid a solid outline, use
curving stems of flowers.*

*Make sure that you criss-cross
the first stems inside the vase to
provide a support for the next set of
stems that you add, and remember
to keep the arrangement topped
up with clean water.*

2 Add stems of larkspur and golden
rod, one on each side of the
vase, at the halfway point between the
gladiolus forming the top and the stock
and lady's mantle at the bottom of the
arrangement. By adding these you have
now set the overall size and shape of
your arrangement.

3 Take the remaining flowers and
infill the body of the arrangement
until there are no empty holes left in
the centre of the urn, and no floral
foam is visible. Be careful not to crowd
together the stems of the flowers.

Fireplace arrangement

LIKE THEIR STUART PREDECESSORS, the Georgians did not care for dark cavernous spaces when the fire was not lit. This decoration was meant to impress, though this may not always have pleased guests as several diarists of the period noted that they had to suffer cold rooms during chilly weather when their hostess used a fireplace arrangement.

The fashion for bough pots, vases large enough to hold branches of flowers and foliage, still thrived. However, as coal replaced logs as the main fuel for domestic fires, so the fashion for hob grates gained popularity in the late eighteenth century. This meant that smaller vases had to be balanced, sometimes precariously, on the new fixed grate, rather than sitting safely on the flat surface of the hearth.

Thoroughly soak the floral foam and tape the blocks securely into the inner waterproof container so that the foam is just below the edge of the rim of the basket. This means that all the stems come up out of the basket rather than hang over the edge. Infill between the inside of the wire basket and the outside of the inner water-proof container with your dried moss to disguise the inner workings.

Set the overall shape of the arrangement by placing a stem of mallow just slightly off centre at the back of the foam, and adding a stem of feverfew at the bottom right edge of the basket with another stem of mallow at the corresponding left-hand side and a short stem of lady's mantle near the centre of the edge of the container Next add a tall stem of lady's mantle on the left side and another stem of mallow on the right to give the overall width.

2 Infill the centre and side points between the starting three stems, leaving a delicate edge to the arrangement so that it does not appear to have a solid outline.

Continue adding the stems until no foam is visible, trying to ensure that each bloom can be seen individually and that the flowers are not crushed together.

TIPS

You may decide against using floral foam as the base, but instead inserting some chicken wire into the container to act as a support for the stems. Pour sufficient water into the container that it is over half full, and top up regularly. Change the water by sweeping the flowers up into a bunch and putting them into another, slightly smaller vase while you wash and refill the main container. By using the slightly smaller vase as a temporary home, the shape of the arrangement can be retained more neatly, and you can then transfer the stems into the clean container and let them fall gently back into their original position.

Mantel vases

FLOWERS AND MATERIALS

a selection of flowers, including
   spray roses, feverfew, love-in-a-
   mist, cornflowers, lady's mantle,
   larkspur buds, sweet peas,
3 Wedgwood Jasperware vases
scissors

FASHIONABLE GEORGIAN HOMES would have displayed small bud vases of flowers on the mantelpiece. These tended to be in odd numbers – as many as thirteen vases have been recorded. They were filled with small bloomed flowers and, whilst the flowers were arranged in an informal and haphazard manner, the vases themselves were placed with strict symmetry in mind. The end vases would have been lined up with the pilasters supporting the mantelshelf.

▌ Remove all lower foliage from the stems to prevent the water turning slimy. Fill each vase three quarters full of water and place them in the sequence in which they will ultimately be displayed, varying the heights of the vases in a symmetrical pattern.

2 Add the stems of the flowers to the vases, ensuring that no two match in contents. Keep a light and natural style to the flowers, so that they do not appear to have been formally arranged, with taller stems to the back and shorter to the sides and front.

TIPS

Before starting to fill the vases with the flowers, check the chimneypiece to see what space there is between the mantel-shelf and any pictures or mirrors hanging above. This will avoid pollen damaging the paintings or covering up detailed plasterwork.

Change the water in the vases every other day during hot weather, and use a non-abrasive scourer or nylon bottle brush to clean the insides of the vases. Thoroughly dry the base of each vase before putting it in its final position to avoid water marks on the mantelshelf.

Kissing bough

FOLIAGE AND MATERIALS

selection of foliage (bay, Scots
pine, conifer, laurel, holly, yew,
variegated holly, fruiting ivy)
red berries
mistletoe
4 firm red apples
2 metres *(2 yards)* red velvet
ribbon
wire ties or string
wooden skewers
4 candles
scissors
secateurs
2 hanging baskets
3 blocks floral foam
rope or chain
floral tape

THIS ARRANGEMENT is a celebration of evergreens, fertility (represented by the red fruits and berries) and the hope of spring to come symbolised by the light of the candles. In its simplest form it can be just a tied bunch of foliage and berries which is hung as a focal piece in a prominent place. The introduction of the Christmas tree in the nineteenth century resulted in a sharp decline in popularity for this decoration, which once enjoyed pride of place in most homes.

To prepare your candles for use, take a length of floral tape and stick one end of the tape to the candle, approx. 5cm (2ins) from the bottom of the candle. Cut two wooden skewers in half and hold the stick parallel to the candle whilst sticking the tape down firmly around the candle. Add one stick at a time and wrap over firmly with the tape. This technique will help you securely to position your candles into the arrangement, as the wooden skewers will slide well down into the floral foam and hold your candles upright.

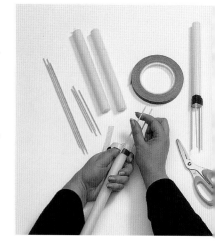

2 Cut your floral foam to fit inside one of the hanging baskets, and firmly fix the baskets together using the wire ties (if you do not have wire ties, you can tie the baskets together with string). Attach your rope into the centre of the top basket (fairly precisely centring of the rope will make it easier for you to hang the basket upright later). Hang the frame up using the rope, and secure. Attach the end of a piece of ribbon to a wooden skewer

using some floral tape, push the skewer into the top centre of the basket, and wrap the ribbon loosely around the rope, taping it to the top of the rope to finish off neatly.

Position your candles in the top basket by pushing the ends of the wooden skewers firmly into the floral foam. It is not recommended that you light these candles, but if you intend to do so, then ensure that they are not so close to the rope that they set it alight!

Set the overall shape and size of your arrangement by putting in a piece of foliage at the very top of the basket, a piece each side of the baskets for the width, a piece in the centre of the basket, and a shorter piece at the bottom of the basket. Now all you have to do is infill with foliage between these starting pieces to keep the overall shape intact.

3 Carry on infilling with your foliage until you can no longer see the floral foam, taking care to stay within the boundaries of your first pieces of foliage so that you keep a good even shape to the arrangement. Support the basket frame with one hand as you push the stems in place, and ensure that the stems are securely held by the floral foam so that no boughs fall out later. Check all angles of the arrangement to ensure that you have no gaps on the opposite side from your starting point. Keep turning the basket round to ensure an even balance to all sides.

4 Finally, add your stems of berries and then the apples. I have secured mine in position by pushing a wooden skewer into the apple and then wiring this skewer firmly into the floral foam at the base of the arrangement.

TIPS

To ensure that the birds don't make a feast of all your holly berries and leave you to resort to artificial ones, just cut some boughs of berried holly in late November or early December, and stand the cut stem ends into a bucket of damp sand. Cover the stems with an old tea towel or blanket and leave it somewhere cool. The damp sand, as opposed to a bucket of water, will ensure that the stems don't rot or become stagnant. The cool temperature will ensure that the berries look fresh when you need them in late December. The cloth will stop the birds from getting to the berries if the bucket is standing outside, and gives some protection from the frost.

One advantage of using artificial berries is that they won't drop and get trodden into the carpet. You may also

consider using artificial apples that can be easily wired into the frame of the hanging basket, will incur less weight and won't run the risk of becoming soft and dropping onto the heads of guests!

Condition your foliage by cutting it the day before you intend to make the arrangement, removing the lower foliage and putting it into a bucket of tepid water, in a cool place.

It is not advisable to light candles in your kissing bough as lit candles should never be left unattended, and may be difficult to extinguish quickly when hung well above head level.

Take care to ensure that the hook or fitting from which you will hang your kissing bough can take the not inconsiderable combined weight of the wet floral foam, foliage and fruit.

Your arrangement will take a huge drink from the floral foam during the first 24 hours, so you may prefer to hang it outside, away from any frost, for a day before putting it in its final position. To keep it looking fresh for longer, water it every couple of days and mist spray it every day. You may find it easiest to water the arrangement with a long-spouted can in the evening, and leave a basin beneath it overnight to catch any excess water that may drain out.

Victorian
extravagance

The Victorians loved flowers with strong scents, so I have included in my selection jasmine and roses. They used a lot of ferns and foliage for arrangements; those shown here include asparagus, maidenhair, leather leaf and ladder ferns, along with camellia leaves, ivy and a very fashionable multi-coloured begonia leaf. In hothouses, the Victorians could grow orchids and oriental lilies. Other flowers include the iris, snowdrop, grape hyacinth, viola, hellebore, primula, tulip, polyanthus and cyclamen, all of which would have had their meanings for Victorians, who built up an elaborate language.

VICTORIAN EXTRAVAGANCE

When Queen Victoria came to the throne at the age of eighteen in 1837, she presented a very different image from her disreputable Hanoverian uncles – demure, pure, and full of romantic idealism. Her marriage three years later to her cousin, Albert of Saxe-Coburg, also ushered in an age that celebrated family values, at least in public. In terms of style, this meant a turning away from the elegance and sparseness of Georgian interiors, and a move towards abundance. The Industrial Revolution had made possible mass production of what had been luxury items, such as furniture and furnishings. Houses were built on a large scale, with rooms for every activity. No longer was furniture ranged along walls to be brought into the centre of the room when needed for eating: instead wealthy Victorian families could enjoy the luxury of not only a dining room, but a breakfast room and a tearoom as well.

This was the age of clutter. Photographs of fashionable Victorian interiors show them to have been incredibly crowded, with every available surface covered with objects. Furniture was heavy and ornate, walls were papered, carpets and window drapes were thick and made in dark and rich colours that absorbed the light. The Drawing Room at Calke Abbey in Derbyshire, little altered since 1856, conveys well this suffocating atmosphere.

It was also the age of eclecticism. The Georgians had oscillated between classical and gothic, but the Victorians took this one stage further, reviving styles from every period of history. When George Hammond Lucy inherited the dilapidated Tudor mansion of Charlecote Park in Warwickshire, he set about refurbishing it in what he perceived as sixteenth-century style. At Knightshayes Court in Devon, William Burges designed a house in the French Gothic style for the Heathcoat Amory family, although his medieval fantasies were never to be properly realised as his patrons reacted in horror to his extraordinary designs and sacked him. The slate magnate G.H.Dawkins Pennant commissioned a neo-Norman castle at Penrhyn in North Wales: the architect Thomas Hopper applied this unlikely style to carpets, sofas and even water-closets.

Among the ornaments that filled these houses were flowers and potted plants. The mound or pyramid were the fashionable shapes, both for the training of plants and the display of cut flowers. Conservatories, also known as Winter Rooms, provided fresh flowers throughout the year, and the Victorians were masters at forcing flowers and fruits to suit the dictates of fashion. In wealthy households, it was the head gardener who made the floral decorations under the supervision of the lady of the house, who might merely advise on where the displays should be placed. In more modest households, where domestic staff were retained for the laborious chores, gardening and flower-arranging were regarded as suitable pursuits for the female members of the family. Ferns and palms were considered the epitome of good taste, larger plants standing on the floors, and smaller pots on side tables and mantelpieces. No well-dressed parlour or drawing room would have been complete without an aspidistra, also known as the cast-iron plant because it was considered virtually indestructible by even the most hopeless of gardeners.

Flowers were used in abundance to decorate dress: corsages for bodices and bonnets, dainty garlands for sleeve caps and frills on skirts, sprays of flowers in the hair, posies and bouquets to be carried. Anemones and tulips were favourites for posies and gown decorations to take to a ball. They would stay tightly budded during the cold, dark drive but would burst into their full glory amidst the heat and bright lights of the ballroom. Camellias were also favoured for personal adornment as they were said to 'withstand much waltzing', although the Victorians would have found their lack of scent a drawback: heavily perfumed flowers such as violets and gardenias were much admired.

As with their interior decoration, the Victorians liked strong colours in flowers, especially in the patterned arrangements that were so fashionable. Blue shades were avoided for most rooms as they were thought to appear

right: The Drawing Room at Calke Abbey, Derbyshire

above: Detail of the Dining Room of Penrhyn Castle in North Wales, with the table laid as for a supper given in July 1894 during a royal visit.

left: A settle in the Drawing Room at Red House, Bexleyheath

dingy under gaslight, but were perfectly acceptable in morning or breakfast rooms which enjoyed an abundance of natural light. A combination of red and white flowers signified unity until the middle of the century when British troops were fighting in the Crimea. Losses totalling more than 45,000 men and the life-saving efforts of Florence Nightingale were widely publicised. Red and white flowers came to represent 'blood and bandages', and to this day these colours are not a welcome combination in many hospitals.

The Victorians developed the symbolism of flowers into a complex language. For instance, if a flower was presented with its leaves intact, this represented affirmity to the sentiment being expressed, while a stripped stem

conveyed the negative. Presenting a flower to the right hand would provide an affirmative response to a question. If a flower was worn on the head, it would convey caution, on the breast, friendship or remembrance, and over the heart, love. For further meanings of flowers for the Victorians, see pp.136-141.

Inevitably the extravagant abundance in interior decoration provoked reaction. Industrialisation had produced a mass of poorly designed products, and designers began to look back to the qualities of hand-made ornament produced by craftsmen. In 1859, William Morris, twenty-five years old and newly married, commissioned the young architect Philip Webb to build him a house in Bexleyheath just to the south of London. Inspired by the vernacular cottages and barns of the Sussex Weald, Webb produced Red House, a plain L-shaped building around a central hall. Morris wanted to fill it with hand-crafted furnishings and furniture that harked back to the Middle Ages, but could not find what he wanted, so that he and his Pre-Raphaelite friends

above: The Drawing Room, Charlecote Park in Warwickshire, furnished and decorated in the Elizabethan Revival Style. The ebony settee in the foreground was bought as a piece of Tudor furniture; in fact, it is seventeenth century and comes from the East Indies.

designed dressers, beds, candlesticks and textiles themselves. This was the beginning of the furnishing firm that was later known as Morris & Co. With the critic John Ruskin, William Morris was also to inspire the Arts & Crafts Movement (see p.112). In terms of flowers the ideas promulgated by Morris and his colleagues meant a reaction to tight, symmetrical arrangements, and a move towards natural simplicity, including the use of wild flowers. He recommended simple 'honest' designs for containers, allowing the flowers to be used in keeping with their natural state; for example, tall boughs of garden flowers in plain earthenware jugs or glassware. The key factor was the quality of every element and skill in its use.

Victorian containers

THE VICTORIANS were able to choose from an eclectic range of vases and urns in porcelain, glass, metal and marble. 'Novelty' containers could be shaped into hands, animals, shells, boots and even monuments. Coloured glass was particularly admired.

The trumpet vase first made its appearance in the late 1840s, and by the 1860s had become the fashionable shape. It came in all shapes and sizes from tiny specimens for a single bloom to large vases over 1 metre (3 feet) in height.

To hold flowers in position, glass or pottery 'roses' were provided, although mesh wire could be used. Damp sand and moss also helped to position flowers. Wire spirals could be fitted in a heavy metal base.

Painted china urn

Munstead vases

left: The Victorians made special posy holders in metal, straw-work and even porcelain. This holder, with its arrangement of eucharis, lady's mantle and asparagus fern, would be used at a ball: when the lady was dancing, the posy would hang from a ring around her finger.

Rose-coloured glass vase with interior stem support

Glass trumpet vases

Large trumpet vase

Wedgwood creamware vase

Gilded urn

Glass vase

Porcelain bowl

Soft paste creamware bowl

Painted earthenware vase on plinth

Silver bowl

Glazed pottery jug

Silver rose bowl with pierced lid

Bud vase

Bridal posy

FLOWERS AND MATERIALS

5 stems bridal gladioli
20 stems white carnation
12 pips stephanotis
leather leaf fern
a wet foam posy holder
a bouquet holder or heavy vase
a white lace frill
scissors

TRADITIONAL VICTORIAN BRIDES carried white bridal flowers as a symbol of their purity and innocence, although a mixture of yellow and white would have been considered acceptable by all but the strictest of social arbiters. White and silver had been a popular choice for aristocratic bridal dress in the eighteenth century, but the white gown worn by Queen Victoria at her marriage in 1840 set the style for white weddings. Etiquette at this time advised that the groom provided the bride's bouquet, and in wealthy households the arrangement would be made up by the family's head gardener.

Mid-Victorian bridal posies were often small, round topped and neatly symmetrical, with concentric bands of flowers and a fine lace or paper edging frill. Some of the flowers were wired with stub wire, and a small amount of damp moss was bound at the base of each stem. These wired stems were then pushed through a bunch of moss and bound together, using thin wire. The base of moss ensured that each flower head was supported and held apart from the next. The wired stem ends were then bound to form a handle and often covered with ribbon or inserted into a delicate cone-shaped posy holder. These holders were produced in silver, metal or straw-work and had a pin mechanism which was pushed through the stems into the opposite side to secure them, or sometimes they had jaws that clamped the stems in place.

Most brides wore a head-dress of small blooms, usually incorporating orange blossom, and this could be worn in conjunction with a bonnet and veil. It was, however, considered inappropriate for older brides to wear a circlet of flowers, or for a widow to have bridesmaids when remarrying.

Other popular flowers for bridal posies included roses, eucharis, orchids, gardenias, lily of the valley and jasmine. Ferns were often used as foliage, together with myrtle signifying love or love in absence, and ivy signifying fidelity.

1 Remove all lower foliage from the stems and cut the ends at a sharp 45° angle to provide a good grip on the floral foam. Thoroughly soak the floral foam holder so that it is wet throughout. Slot the handle of the holder through the centre of the lace frill and clamp it into the stand, or stand it upright in a heavy vase.

Start to set the overall shape of the posy by firmly pushing stems of leather leaf fern into the foam holder around the outer edge of the posy. This will set the overall size and symmetrical shape of the posy.

2 Add a ring of short-stemmed carnations above the layer of fern and position a carnation in the centre of the posy.

3 Add a ring of gladioli and small pieces of leather leaf fern around the central carnation. To finish the arrangement, infill the remaining space with a ring of carnations and stephanotis to ensure that no floral foam is visible.

TIPS

You may decide that you would prefer to work from the centre of the arrangement out towards the edges, but this will mean that you have to lift the edges of the previous layer to slot flowers underneath it, possibly resulting in broken flower heads.

Keep turning the posy to face you every so often to check you are achieving overall balance. If the front appears flat when viewed from the side, it means that the central stems are too short. Add a few longer stems to give a gentle curve.

Make the posy the day before it is needed. Ensure that the floral foam is kept moist and the posy mist sprayed with water. Store in a cool room, out of direct sunlight.

To store the posy, take a cardboard box slightly larger in overall size and push the open flaps inside on themselves. Stand the box on the floor, open side down, and make a small hole in the centre with scissors. Slide the handle of the posy holder into the hole and the box will support the outer edges of the bouquet.

Flower basket

FLOWERS AND MATERIALS

12 stems sweet peas
8 sprigs rosemary
6 stems honeysuckle
6 stems pink spray roses
4 stems pink roses
6 sprigs myrtle
5 stems daisies
5 stems lily of the valley
5 stems pinks
plastic-lined basket
wet floral foam
stub wires
serrated scissors

A DELICATE basket of flowers might be carried by young girls on social occasions, including as bridesmaids. Young bridesmaids often carried white flowers in keeping with those of the bride, although it was permissible to include flowers in shades to complement their dresses. Older bridesmaids were more likely to carry a bouquet than a basket of flowers.

The flowers chosen here all had meanings for the Victorians, who built up an elaborate language to convey their sentiments (see pp.136-141). Lily of the valley carried the promise of happiness, white rosebuds suggested ignorance of love, myrtle conveyed love in absence. Rosemary had for centuries been associated with both weddings and funerals, as it was symbol of the affairs of the heart as well as of remembrance.

The rosemary and myrtle would have been arranged around the outside of the basket to brush against skirts and release the aromatic fragrance. Ivy-leafed geraniums were not recommended for edging as they were considered to give a sickly smell if the leaves were damaged.

1 Use a piece of plastic to line your basket, so that no water can escape through the open weave of the willow. Place a small block of wet foam in the basket and secure it into place by pushing pieces of hairpin-shaped stub wires through the weave.

2 Start to set the shape of the arrangement by placing your foliage around the edge of the basket, taking care to leave some room for the bearer's hands to grasp the handle comfortably.

3 Add your flowers to ensure an even balance of colour and texture. If some of the stems are too delicate to push straight into the foam, just take a small, sturdy stem and start a hole in the foam before pushing in the delicate stem.

4 Keep the basket of flowers in a cool place and mist spray with water. Do not overfill the foam with water, as this will slosh about in the bottom of the basket, and possibly splash out onto the bearer's gown.

ALTERNATIVE FLOWER SUGGESTIONS

bourbon roses	snowdrops	camellias
stephanotis	violets	tulips
fuchsia heads	pansies	hellebores
small-headed gladioli	small-headed irises	forget-me-nots
carnations	peonies	

Bridal corsage and head-dress

FLOWERS AND MATERIALS

For the head-dress
5 sprigs orange blossom
6 white rosebuds
9 jasmine pips
3 heads white bridal gladioli
2 stems asparagus fern
reel wire
stub wire
stem wrap
serrated scissors

For the corsage
3 stems white rosebud
3 sprigs orange blossom
2 stems lily of the valley
3 sprigs jasmine foliage
5 jasmine pips
1 stem asparagus fern
reel wire
stub wire
stem wrap
serrated scissors

IN THE 1850S and '60s, brides and their bridesmaids decorated their crinoline gowns with corsages worn at the waist or on the neckline. Doubled up, the arrangement could be worn on the head as a wreath.

It was, however, important to remember that the head is a source of heat, so the head gardener would advise the lady's maid dressing the bride to ensure that the head-dress was put in position at the very last moment to prevent delicate flowers and foliage from wilting. One method of ensuring that a head-dress looked fresh for longer was to wrap the individual flowers in pieces of damp cotton wool or moss. The resulting bundle could be wrapped in another piece of cotton wool and secured with a piece of thin wire. The Victorians would then add a couple of drops of isinglass onto the outer cotton wool to stick down the outer petals of the flowers and avoid shedding.

The most popular flower for Victorian bridal wreaths was orange blossom. It has been suggested that the orange traditionally represented the golden apple of classical mythology, presented as a gift by Jupiter to Juno on their wedding day. It also has connections with fertility, as the orange tree was thought to produce far more fruit if some of its blossom was removed after first flowering.

Make the corsage in the same way as making half of the head-dress, but disguise the wired stem ends by stem wrapping an inverted wired leaf to finish off.

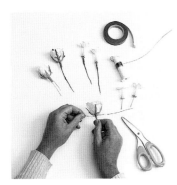

I Wire each flower separately using fine reel or stub wires. Push the wire through the stem, just below the flower head, and then pull the wire down parallel with the stem itself. Use stem wrap to tidy up the appearance of the wired stem and, more importantly, to seal the moisture inside the stem to prolong the life of the flower.

2 Wire each leaf by pushing a piece of wire through the back of the leaf itself, about halfway up. Draw both ends of the wire down parallel with the stem and wrap the stem as above.

3 Stem wrap two pieces of thick stub wire, approx. 12-15cm (5-6 inches) long to make a base. Stem wrap each piece and then make a very small loop on one end of each piece of wire (this enables the wearer to use a hair grip to secure the head-dress into position). Start to stem wrap the individual stems of smaller foliage and flowers onto one end of the pieces of base wire, starting at the end with the small loop, to build up a tapering shape. Lay the stems against the base wire working in the same direction, using the heads of the flowers to cover

the stems of the previous flower, gradually building the head-dress into a thicker shape, and using larger, more solid flowers in the centre as you travel along the base wire. Leave at least 2.5cm (1 inch) of the end of the base wire free of flowers as this is where you will need to join the two pieces of wire together by overlapping them and stem wrapping them together. Repeat the process with the second piece of wire.

4 To join both sections of the head-dress, hold them in the centre and tightly wire and then stem wrap them together, making sure that they are firmly joined.

ALTERNATIVE FLOWER SUGGESTIONS

camellias	spray roses
white orchids	gardenias
orange blossom	

Concentric dish arrangement

FLOWERS AND MATERIALS

9 open ivory oriental lily heads
8 clusters pink scented pelargoniums
3 stems cream spray roses
6 stems fern
16 large ivy leaves
a plastic floral bowl
2 blocks wet floral foam
floral tape
scissors

THE VICTORIANS' love of symmetry and precision is amply demonstrated in these formal arrangements which, at the height of their popularity in the 1860s, might have graced the side tables of fashionable homes.

Suitable containers for this arrangement included a single tier cake stand on a foot, a low bowl, a large saucer or a soup bowl. A domed pile of damp sand (not too wet to avoid slumping) would have been used, covered by a layer of dampened moss in which the flowers and foliage were inserted.

By the 1870s, the popularity of concentric bands was on the wane. Instead, it was suggested that small bundles of a single variety of flowers should be dotted amongst greenery, or whole potted plants could be arranged in a less structured form in this shape of bowl, a glass or wicker basket, or on a saucer.

1 Thoroughly soak the floral foam and cut the blocks to fit inside the bowl in a domed shape. Fix securely with floral tape. Add twelve of the large ivy leaves at a slightly upward angle around the rim of the bowl so that they hang down, covering the edge of the container. This has now set the overall size of the arrangement.

2 Cut the fern into small pieces and add a layer of fern above the ivy leaves. Position eight heads of oriental lily above the fern so that they are just touching one another but are not squashed together. Position another layer of small pieces of fern above the lily heads. Add a ring of the pelargonium flowers above this, followed by a further ring of fern.

3 Finish the arrangement by adding one last layer of fern and the four remaining ivy leaves to form a border containing the cream spray roses, and lastly a central lily head.

TIPS

You may prefer to work from the centre outwards, but this will mean you have to lift the previous layer slightly to slot in the layer beneath, which can result in broken flower heads.

When using lilies, it is always a good idea to remove the pollen stamens (see p.125).

To water successfully, place your fingers just inside the bowl's reservoir and gently pour water into the arrangement near the centre. As the reservoir fills up, the water level will touch your fingers before it reaches the outer rim of the container, so you will know when it is full.

ALTERNATIVE ARRANGEMENTS

pink oriental lilies
cineraria
honeysuckle
variegated ivy leaves
leather leaf fern
pink sweet peas
pink rose

variegated ivy leaves
leather leaf fern
scabious
delphiniums
cineraria
pink carnations
cream spray roses

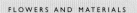

Pyramid mound arrangement

FLOWERS AND MATERIALS

18 stems pink heather
16 fuchsia heads
10 passion flower heads
4 stems lady's mantle
2 stems mallow
block of floral foam
vase with a plinthed
foot
sharp knife
scissors

THIS POPULAR nineteenth-century arrangement was made on a 'Pyramid Bouquet Stand' invented by Daniel Stead of Huddersfield in Yorkshire. The stand consisted of a pyramidal cylinder of metal with a series of pierced holes at regular intervals. Inside was another, slightly smaller cylinder which contained a tube that could be filled with water. The stems of the flowers, only a few centimetres/an inch long, were inserted into the holes in the outer case and were supported by the inner cylinder from which they drew a small amount of water by capillary action.

Flowers in this container were said to last up to a fortnight as the stems were not submerged as with a standard vase. Garden flowers could thus be used to best effect without denuding even a small garden. A single bough of flowers could be cut down into many small sections to fill the cylinder. In *Rustic Adornments for Homes of Taste* published in 1856, James Shirley Hibberd recommended garden flowers for the arrangement. These included a stand full of scarlet pelargoniums, a mixture of asters, pansies and verbenas, chrysanthemums in rows of single colours, or a mass of pansies with a row of white asters at the base.

Shirley Hibberd's book was largely aimed at the fast growing and prosperous middle classes of Victorian Britain, and was one of the first of such publications dealing with the all-important matters of the day, refinement and good taste. Whereas the head gardener would still be responsible for arranging the flowers in an upper-class household, young ladies and married women of the middle classes were actively encouraged to take an interest in the choice, construction and display of flowers and plants in the home, as well as in the wider interests of gardening.

1 Shape the floral foam carefully and wedge firmly into the base of the vase. To avoid using two blocks if your vase is very deep, put a small, water-proof container inside the top of the vase to give more height to the foam. The danger of using two blocks pegged together is that the top block will dry out quickly and be difficult to re-water.

2 Start by arranging the largest flower heads, pushing the cut stem ends firmly into the foam. As a rule of thumb, use larger flowers towards the base and slightly smaller flowers nearer the top so that the arrangement does not become top heavy.

Infill with the smaller flower heads until no foam is visible. Try not to crush the heads together.

TIPS

Keep turning the vase every so often as you work, to check that you are achieving an overall balance and symmetry.

Remember to water the arrangement from the top as well as the vase itself to ensure that the upper part of the floral foam stays damp.

ALTERNATIVE ARRANGEMENTS

11 red roses

30 heads cream-yellow spray
  chrysanthemums

12 sprays clove-coloured carnations

1 stem blue gentian

*This arrangement is in concentric
bands, a popular style in the 1860s
(see pp.92-3).*

12 red roses
10 stems daisies
18 stems pink heather
16 fuchsia heads
6 short stems jasmine

March stand

THOMAS MARCH, a civil servant working in the Lord Chamberlain's Office, caused a storm at the Royal Horticultural Society's show in London in 1861 with his flower stand. This was made of glass, with the possibility of extensions to allow up to three tiers of arrangements to be 'tastefully displayed'. It won first prize over the 'lumpish' style of table decorations that had previously been considered fashionable.

Mr March suggested combinations of ordinary garden flowers that could be shown to pleasing effect, offering detailed instructions into methods of arranging in his book, *Flower and Fruit Decoration*, published in 1862. He suggested that seven stems of a large flower should be used in the bottom tier and five large flower heads in the upper tier, with the flowers forming evenly placed, concentric bands. Smaller flowers, such as spray roses, should be placed in greater number, but still in a symmetrical pattern.

As the original stands were made of glass, few have survived. I have recreated this design by using a tall, sturdy candlestick. The construction of the arrangement would originally have been in dishes using a base of damp sand or clay covered with moss. For longevity in modern surroundings, I have recreated this display using wet floral foam.

1 Press some floral fix around the outside of the candle plate, as this will secure your top dish firmly in place without the need for extra floral tape around the stem of the candlestick. Take care not to impale yourself on the candle spike at this stage!

2 Using a drill or bradawl, carefully make a small hole in the middle of the top dish to allow it to sit neatly over the candle spike. Place a piece of cork beneath the dish as you pierce the hole, to avoid cracking the dish or marking any surface beneath it.

3 Cut your floral foam and securely tape it into position by sticking the end of the tape onto the bottom of the saucer and then pulling it over the floral foam before sticking it firmly to the bottom of the container on the other side (floral tape sticks to most things apart from the floral foam!). Place your candlestick in the centre of your large plant saucer and then lay two-thirds of a block of floral foam against each of the three legs, wedging the remaining one-third of each in between the large section to fill the rest of the saucer. Tape this securely in place. Firmly press the small top dish onto the metal candle plate, again carefully navigating the candle spike.

Push the cut stem end of the jasmine into the floral foam at the centre of the bottom tray, wind the foliage up the candlestick and then cut the top of the stem, anchoring it into the floral foam in the top dish. Add your snowdrops into the centre of the top dish and the centre of the lower dish, around the candlestick. As the stems of snowdrops are soft, you may find it helpful to make a small hole in the floral foam with a twig of sturdier stem, and then insert your soft-stemmed flowers.

4 Set the shape of your arrangements using your foliage by taking the leather leaf fern and cutting each stem into several short sections. Push the stems of this foliage into the foam all the way round the outer edge of each tray to form a wide fringe. Next add a short stem of leather leaf in the centre of the top dish and of the bottom dish so that it is slightly lower than the snowdrops. Add the asparagus fern at an upward angle into the top tray so that it droops down over the edges of the tray and conceals the metal candle plate. Now infill with your foliage between the tallest and lowest pieces of foliage in your top dish, and repeat in the bottom tray, keeping a smooth shape to the arrangements. Continue to add foliage until you can hardly see the floral foam.

TIPS

By cutting the floral foam to fit the edges of the dishes, you can still insert flowers with shorter stems to the edges of your display.

When watering your arrangements, put your finger inside the edge of the dish so that you can feel the water level and do not overfill the container. Mist spray your arrangement every day, and remove and replace any fading flowers.

5 Cutting the stems quite short, add a well-spaced ring of irises to the bottom tier, roughly positioning them at the edge of the plant saucer. Next add the five stems of iris to the top tier, following the same principle.

6 Lastly add the spray roses, again following a concentric pattern and spacing them equally throughout the arrangements to form a band of colour between the irises and the snowdrops.

ALTERNATIVE ARRANGEMENTS

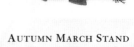

LILY MARCH STAND

same containers, foam and tools as
   on p.98
same foliage plus 12 variegated
   ivy leaves
13 red roses
12 stems honeysuckle
20 sprays mock orange
6 stems pink spray roses
8 stems small-headed hebe
1 long trailing piece of honeysuckle

CHRISTMAS MARCH STAND

same containers, foam and tools as
   on p.98
same foliage plus 12 variegated
   ivy leaves and 12 stems fir
12 stems red carnations
15 stems gilded cones (see p.11)
2 metres (2 yards) ribbon for loops
1 metre (1 yard) ribbon for central
   support

AUTUMN MARCH STAND

same containers, foam and tools as
   on p.98
same foliage plus 12 variegated
   ivy leaves
4 stems bronze spray chrysanthemums,
5 stems cream lisianthus

Pot à fleur

FLOWERS AND MATERIALS

begonia
snowdrop
jasmine
nephrolepsis
grape hyacinths
2 primulas
maidenhair fern
variegated ivies
1 asparagus fern
dragon palm *(dracaena)*
plastic-lined basket
gravel

Other suitable foliage plants:
ficus, kangaroo, vine, agaves, yucca
plants, ferns

Other suitable flowering plants:
hyacinths, lilies, chrysanthemums,
spiraeas, orchids

THIS IS AN ARRANGEMENT of pots of foliage plants interspersed with flowering plants that can be changed to provide year-round colour.

Groups of plants were often used to decorate nineteenth-century homes, particularly as summer decoration in fireplaces, and as year-round features for corners of rooms and the base of staircases. This decoration consisted of a tub or trough (often wooden, enamelled zinc or wire stands) filled with a selection of foliage plants. To this an ever-changing series of flowering plants could be added and removed after flowering to provide a colour contrast to the base foliage.

Line your baskets with plastic and then add a generous amount of gravel to the base of each. Start to add your main plants (largest features) to establish an outline shape for your display.

2 Continue filling in any places with the smaller flowering plants, taking care that you cannot see any pots though the foliage. If you have any awkward spaces left, you can always add a little moss to fill up the gaps, and this will also mulch the plants to help keep them moist.

TIPS

I have taken moss from my lawn, which has a far greater moss to grass ratio than strictly fashionable. Otherwise, it is easily available from garden centres or florist shops. Do not be tempted to harvest your own from common land or parks, as not only would this be hugely detrimental to the local environment, but you could also be liable for a considerable fine if caught!

Round containers work really well on landings or at the base of stairs, whereas rectangular or square containers are often better in fireplaces. Choose shade-tolerant plants for dark corners. Mist spraying and regular feeding will keep the plants in tip-top condition. Remove sad-looking plants for a well-earned rest in the greenhouse before returning them to another arrangement.

Everlasting flower arrangement

FLOWERS AND MATERIALS

8 heads preserved roses
½ bunch helichrysum
8 stems hops
6 stems dried fern
6 stems preserved beech
15 stems love-lies-bleeding
¼ bunch love-in-a-mist seed pods
scissors
floral tape
a vase
block of dry floral foam

EVERLASTING FLOWERS, or immortelles as they were also known, were hugely popular in Victorian Britain, and were often used in wreaths, crosses and bouquets, as well as in arrangements in vases. The last were usually displayed on mantelshelves or on drawing-room tables. They were often covered with a glass dome or crystal shade to protect them from the dust and 'other impurities', and could last in all their loveliness for several years. The collection, drying and arranging of flowers was suggested to be a most suitable hobby for young ladies.

Dried materials that were readily available to buy or easy to dry in the home included: fern fronds, autumnal foliage of oak maple, roses, pelargoniums, grasses, acroclinium, helichrysum, *helipterum sandfordii*, rhodanthe daisies, xeranthemums, *gomphrena globosa*, *phoenocoma prolifera*, ammobium, *aphelexis purpurea*, statice, gypsophila, skeletonised leaves (shadow leaves), and seed pods.

Some of these varieties are no longer commercially grown, but can be grown from seed that is available.

Dried flowers and foliage were often used in Christmas decorations to add colour and texture to the base of ubiquitous evergreens.

▐ Cut the floral foam and fit it snugly into the vase, leaving it slightly taller than the rim so that the flowers hang down to cover the tape and other materials. Secure the foam in place with floral tape. If the china vase is cold, the tape will not stick to the surface, so wrap it around the neck of the vase several times so that the tape adheres to itself and you get a firm grip.

Place a tall stem of foliage in the centre of the floral foam, towards the back of the vase. Add a piece of foliage to hang over the rim at the left- and right-hand sides.

2 Infill the diagonals of the vase by adding a piece of foliage (slightly shorter than the first leading stem) in the centre of the vase, followed by pieces on either side of the main top stem. This will set the overall height, width and depth of the arrangement. By keeping inside these stem lengths you will create an even-shaped arrangement.

3 Add the stems of flowers, ensuring that the blooms are closely packed but not crushed together. Use the larger stems in the centre of the arrangement, and the narrower, taller stems towards the edges so that the outline is soft and light.

TIPS

To air dry flowers and foliage, cut them on a dry day, bind into small bunches (the maximum, 20 stems at a time) and hang them upside down in a well-ventilated room out of direct sunlight to prevent the colour bleaching away. The faster the flowers dry, the better the lasting colour. By hanging the flowers upside down, the stems should dry relatively straight, although some flowers, such as hydrangeas, dry well late in the season if they are put in a vase with several inches of water when first cut. The small amount of water stops them flopping, and when the water runs out, they will start to dry, and should be completely dry within a couple of weeks.

Single blooms can be dried easily in sand or silica crystal, though flowers dried in silica will absorb moisture when removed from the compound, and are best displayed in rebated shadow boxes behind glass.

Many flowers can be dried quickly in the microwave, but take care to dry the flowers, not cook them till they burn!

Keep the power on low and set the timer for a few seconds at a time. Check to see how warm the petals have become and repeat until the flower is dry.

Some flowers will dry out even in water, eg.lady's mantle, rhodanthe daisy, gypsophila, statice and helichrysum.

To dye dried flowers, cut the stems and stand them in a mixture of food dye and water. You will see the stem change colour as the dye is drawn up.

To preserve foliage with glycerine so that it remains supple, stand the cut stems in a mixture of two parts of hot water to one part of glycerine in a warm room, out of direct light. You can also use this method on flowers that tend to become brittle, such as gypsophila, lavender and hydrangeas. The process can take up to five weeks or so, depending on the heat of the room and the volume of foliage to be preserved. If you find that the natural colour distorts too greatly, next time try adding food dye into the glycerine and water mixture, or use a floral paint aerosol and spray the foliage when it is fully preserved. You will find that fluffy textures such as gypsophila take paint far more effectively when preserved with glycerine as they do not clog up.

Christmas mantelpiece decorations

FLOWERS AND MATERIALS

selection of foliage, including fir, holly,
   ivy, berries
preserved red roses and seed pods
   (see p.105)
a length of plastic to cover the mantle
gilded cones (see p.11)
3 metres (3 yards) red velvet ribbon
3 metres (3 yards) tartan ribbons
3 blocks of wet floral foam and tape
bunch of stub wires
plastic trays (each to hold a single
   block of foam)
scissors
secateurs

THE VICTORIANS really went to town on their celebrations at Christmas. Boughs of evergreen decorated even the most modest of homes, while wealthier families arranged swags of foliage around picture frames, columns, doorways, staircases, over mirrors and mantelpieces and along sideboards. Popular foliage included branches of fir, laurel, ivy, holly, arbutus, snowberries, ferns and laurustinus. Box was used for smaller decorations. Cut flowers available at this time of the year included camellias, gardenias, hyacinths, calanthes, cinerarias, and chrysanthemums. Also available from hothouses were orchids, white lilac, arum lilies, rosebuds, violets and bouvardias.

During the nineteenth century, it became fashionable to use everlasting and immortelle flowers and preserved autumn foliage to supplement the fresh evergreens (see p.104).

Mantels would probably have been decorated by making a long garland of foliage bound onto a rope and damp moss base (see pp.42-3) with flowers wired amongst the foliage. If the garlands were made by wiring bundles of foliage into a base and interspersed with flowers, then the flowers could easily be replaced as they faded.

Bearing in mind the modern elements of double glazing, central heating – and lack of a large number of servants to replace the arrangements! – I have reconstructed this traditional mantelpiece decoration using trays of floral foam, which can be watered easily. By using a base of hardy foliage with preserved flowers, combined with regular watering and a bit of 'titivating', this arrangement can last for up to a month.

Cover the mantelpiece with a layer of plastic to protect it from water damage by cutting a bin bag down both sides to form a long rectangle and fold it to fit the size of the shelf. Lap it slightly up to the wall to protect paintwork and wallpaper. Thoroughly soak the floral foam and tape it securely into the plastic trays. Place one tray in the middle of the shelf with the others on either side.

Start to set the overall shape of the arrangement by placing a tall stem in the centre of the middle block, towards the back. Add a trailing piece of foliage at either end of the outside blocks, a piece at a diagonal angle beneath the tallest stem, and a short stem in the front of the middle block. This will set the outline of the height, length and depth of the arrangement.

2 Working from the two ends back towards the middle, add diagonally placed stems of foliage to complete the outline.

3 When most of the floral foam has been covered, start to add the flowers. Wire up the ribbons and cones as shown opposite and dot them randomly through the arrangement.

TIPS

If you plan to light the fire beneath the mantelpiece, ensure that you do not leave tendrils of foliage hanging over the front edge of the middle of the fireplace. Mist spraying the arrangement with water will also help to prolong the life of the decoration. Use a large piece of cardboard from a box to slip down behind the arrangement to protect the wall from the water spray.

Ensure that the arrangement is watered adequately every day by placing your fingers into the edge of the tray and watering the floral foam slowly with a long-spouted watering can. You will feel any water rising up to the rim of the trays if you overfill them. You may find it useful to lay a towel beneath the arrangement when watering to catch any excess that may drain out.

If the floral foam is allowed to dry out, it might tip the arrangement off the mantelpiece, as most of the weight of the display will then be directed forward to the edge of the shelf.

The long trails of ribbon at either end of the arrangement were made by cutting 2 metres (2 yards) of each type of ribbon and laying the tartan on top of the red velvet ribbon and finding the centre point. The centre point was pinched together and then securely taped onto the end of a wooden skewer. It was then easy to position the ribbons by pushing the wooden skewer into the end block of floral foam.

Making Wired Bows

Take a piece of ribbon and fold it into a collar (as though you were putting a scarf around your neck). Take the point at which the ribbon meets as it crosses and ruche the centre of the bow together as if you were pleating the fabric. Make a small hook on the end of a piece of stub wire. Place this hook on the centre of the bow and wire it firmly together. Have a go – it really is that easy once you acquire the knack.

Wiring Fir Cones

Turn the fir cone upside down so that the base faces you, take a firm stub wire and hold the end of the wire underneath the lowest open part of the cone. With your other hand run the rest of the wire around the base of the cone under the 'leaves' of the cone, leaving a length of the wire ready for securing the cone later. The wire will disappear inside the leaves and stay invisible when you turn the cone upright.

CHRISTMAS TRADITIONS

The popular myth is that Queen Victoria and Prince Albert introduced the custom of the Christmas tree to Britain. In fact, it was Victoria's grandmother, Charlotte of Mecklenburg -Strelitz who brought her childhood tradition from Germany when she married George III. Victoria and Albert, however, inspired the enduring image of the family decorating their Christmas tree. It is said that the Queen even promoted the custom by presenting fir trees to schools, barracks and public institutions.

Fashionable decorations for trees included patriotic paper flags, beads, paper cones with ribbon handles (containing sweets, nuts, and novelties), candle lights on weighted holders, crackers, glass baubles and paper or fabric flowers.

Edwardian
luxury

Hothouses enabled the Edwardians to grow exotic flowers such as orchids and lilies for their stylised arrangements. Here I have shown the phalaensopsis and cymbidium orchids, and the arum and longiflorum lilies, together with the slightly blowsy roses, peonies and sweet peas that were much admired at this period. But the Edwardians also loved cottage garden flowers with their subtle colours, and I have included in my selection lady's mantle, foxgloves, scabious, lupins, campanula, periwinkle, pinks, sweet Williams and hydrangea.

EDWARDIAN LUXURY

Edward VII reigned for only ten years, from 1901 to 1910, but his influence as a leader of fashion had begun much earlier, when his mother, Queen Victoria, had largely retired from public life. So, we have made this last chapter run from 1880 to 1914 when the lifestyle of the Edwardians came to an abrupt end with the cataclysm of the First World War. This period has been called the last age of elegance. The Edwardians moved away from what they perceived as the stuffiness of all things Victorian, and embraced a new simplicity and 'honesty' of style that was reflected in their taste for fashion, decorating and design.

There were two strands to this taste. First, the devotees of the Arts & Crafts Movement believed that good design could be achieved by the revival of traditional materials and techniques. In addition they proposed that this should apply not only to the design of products, but also to a way of life. These ideals can be seen put into practice at Standen in West Sussex,

a house commissioned by the wealthy London solicitor, James Beale, from Philip Webb in 1892, forty years after producing Red House for William Morris (see pp.82-3). Webb remained true to those early ideals, and provided the Beale family with a good plain building with comfortable interiors furnished by Morris & Co and Arts & Crafts designers such as William de Morgan and W.R.Lethaby. The colours are bold and jewel-like in reds, greens and blues.

The Aesthetic Movement has been described as the younger, more raffish brother of Arts & Crafts. Aesthetes like Walter Pater and Oscar Wilde declared that art was essentially useless, and should be pursued for its own sake. Nevertheless, there were many links between the interior decoration advocated by the Aesthetes and by the Arts & Crafts Movement. The favourite flower of the Aesthetes was the lily auratum, the golden-rayed lily that had been introduced into western Europe in the 1860s when Japan was wrested from its centuries of isolation. Japanese design quickly became very influential on all branches of art, including flower arranging. Moving away from the concentric symmetry and starkly contrasting colours of which the Victorians were so fond, the 'artistic set' developed free-style interpretations including daring displays of twigs, branches of single foliage such as beech, and blossoms in huge pots of oriental design. It was advised that flowers and foliage should be arranged in a manner that was in sympathy with their growing habitat, not stiffly wired or set in clustered bands.

The second stream of fashion was much more conventional – and would have been the style favoured by Edward both as Prince of Wales and then as King. This was the golden age of the English country house, when those with money and leisure could indulge in effortless luxury, with their rounds of weekend parties

left: The fireplace in the Dining Room at Standen, West Sussex. The whole ensemble was designed by the architect Philip Webb.

right: The Saloon at Dunham Massey, Cheshire

above: The White Bedroom at Kingston Lacy, Dorset.

left: The Drawing Room at Standen, West Sussex.

below: The Dining Room at Smallhythe Place, Kent.

arrangements were *de rigueur,* proof that the hostess could afford enough flowers to fill the vase. It was not until the 1930s, when Constance Spry revolutionised flower arranging, that it became acceptable once again to have mixed variety displays.

But the Edwardians also loved cottage garden flowers, with less formal arrangements of water lilies, sweet peas, lily of the valley, stocks, scabious and large, blowsy roses in jugs and bowls. At Smallhythe Place in Kent, the great actress Ellen Terry planted banks of daffodils in the spring and tiers of sweet peas in the summer to provide the house with blooms that she could arrange in simple jugs and vases.

and constant pursuit of pleasure. Like the Aesthetes, country-house owners had moved away from the clutter and hectic patterns and ornamentation of their Victorian predecessors. At Dunham Massey in Cheshire, the decorator Percy Macquoid looked back into history when he was commissioned to refurbish the interior, but took his inspiration from a whole series of sources to produce a comfortable, relaxed atmosphere. His colour palette was softer than Webb's and much more sophisticated than those of the mid-Victorian period. In the Saloon, for instance, he used apple and moss greens with different yellows and browns for the furnishing. For the Summer Parlour he used whites and creams as the backdrop to bright, floral chintzes. This combination is also to be seen in the White Bedroom at Kingston Lacy in Dorset, decorated for the owner and his new bride in 1897.

These light, luxurious rooms provided the setting for stylised flowers such as orchids, large scented lilies and Malmaison carnations, gladioli and Solomon seal displayed in large vases or pots. The development of efficient refrigeration increased the availablity of flowers all year round, and single variety and colour

Edwardian containers

TALL CONTAINERS were particularly fashionable in the late nineteenth and early twentieth centuries for the dramatic flower arrangements. For single blooms, which might decorate the breakfast tray of a house guest, bud or specimen vases were used. Wedgwood vases and Leeds ware (cream-coloured earthenware) enjoyed renewed popularity.

Vases in the Art Nouveau and Art Deco styles were particularly suited to 'aesthetic' arrangements. Gertrude Jekyll designed art glass vases which were named Munstead after her house and famous garden in Surrey.

Twigs or small branches inserted into the tops of vases formed dividers which supported stems, or strips of lead pleated into folds were added to the bottoms of containers for Ikebana style arrangements.

Pewter ewer

Art glass vase

Pottery jug (glazed)

Coronation mug

Art Deco glass bo with pierced

left: A small trumpet vase filled with garden moss. The flowers in the arrangement are *eucharis grandiflora*, snowdrops and maidenhair fern.

Tall glass trumpet
vase

Wedgwood
creamware vase

Glass vase

Silver vase

Wedgwood
Jasperware vases

Creamware bowl

Silver bowl

Copper rose bowl
with pierced lid

Blue and white
ginger jar

Glass trumpet vases

Munstead vases

Bridal bouquet

FLOWERS AND MATERIALS

6 stems ivory roses

5 stems ivory carnations

3 stems *eucharis grandiflora*

10 stems ivory Brompton stocks

5 stems ivory bridal gladioli

10 stems leather leaf fern

10 stems long-stemmed
   asparagus fern

scissors

a wet foam bouquet holder
   (*extra large caged oval*)

a bouquet stand

THE MOST FASHIONABLE bouquets of the early twentieth century tended to be large, loose and unstructured. These included tapering, long arm sheaths and full shower arrangements. Ivory or white flowers were still a firm favourite for the bride's own bouquet. The most popular flowers included roses, carnations, lily of the valley, longiflorum and arum lilies, and for foliage, the ubiquitous ferns.

Bouquets often contained one, or at most two single varieties of flowers, their stems painstakingly wired and then arranged into a shower which must have been heavy and cumbersome to deal with when wearing so many layers of constricting clothing.

  With the developments in floral foam holders, floral glues and reliable stem wrap, bouquets today are rarely wired together. I have used a floral foam holder to make this bouquet so that it is an achievable project for anyone who is new to flower arranging. To make a wired bouquet could be off-putting as it can take many hours of practice and countless trial runs before the technique is perfected. However, a note of caution. If you are planning on making a bridal bouquet, do give yourself enough time to practise with at least one trial run well in advance of the wedding.

  I have used a bouquet stand that clamps the handle of the bouquet holder and holds it at the correct position to work on. If you do not have such a holder, you'll need a very patient friend to hold the bouquet. The alternative is to wrap the handle in cling film, and push it down into a bowl of damp floral foam. The foam will support the bouquet frame, but you will be looking directly down onto the holder, so do pick the holder up every so often to check the arrangement from all angles.

▌ Remove all lower foliage from the stems and cut ends at a sharp 45° angle so that they get a good grip on the foam holder. Thoroughly soak the floral foam holder so that it is wet throughout and then clamp the bouquet holder into the stand. Start to set the overall shape of the bouquet by firmly pushing stems of asparagus fern into the foam holder, one long stem for the drop

of the bouquet, one short stem sticking directly up at the top, and one stem either side to set the width. If you are using heavy stems of flowers or foliage to make long trails at the bottom of the bouquet, you may want to wire them (see p.91). Push the stub wire up through the floral foam holder until it comes out at the top, and then double the wire back into the foam over one of

the plastic cage straps. This will ensure that the long trailing stems cannot work loose.

  Start to infill the diagonal points between the stems of foliage, adding the ferns until little of the floral foam base is still visible. Use shorter stems in the centre of the bouquet and be sure to turn the frame to check that there is no foam visible from either side angle.

2 Start adding the flowers into the base of foliage, using the largest flowers first and then infilling with the smaller blooms. The aim is to achieve a natural balance rather than a precise symmetry to the positioning of the flowers, with some clusters of flowers and some areas of plain greenery.

If you are a beginner, you may feel more confident about positioning the first few pieces of foliage on outside edges to set the shape of the bouquet by adding a dab of floral glue to the part of the stem that sits on the outside plastic edge of the holder. This is not strictly necessary but may help to reassure you that nothing will fall out of the holder later.

Keep turning the bouquet so that you can check that you are achieving the overall balance. If the front appears flat when viewed from the side, it will mean that the central stems are too short. If you add a few longer stems into the centre, you will give a gentle curve to the bouquet.

Make the bouquet the day before it is needed. Ensure the floral foam is kept moist and mist spray the flowers with water. Store in a cool room, out of direct sunlight. To store the bouquet, see p.87.

Wrist corsage and arm sheath

FLOWERS AND MATERIALS

2 open heads ivory oriental lily
1 bud ivory oriental lily
2 metres (2 yards) ivory satin
    ribbon
1 metre (1 yard) ivory ribbon to
    make wrist tie (max.1.25cm
    (1½ in) wide)
serrated scissors
stub wires
stem wrap
clear nylon 'fishing reel'
glue (hot glue gun or floristry glue)

Wrist corsage

THE FORERUNNERS of this decoration were corsages for the bodice, sleeve caps and skirt so loved by the Victorians. The Edwardians' passion for simplicity is reflected in the stylish wrist/arm corsage which could be worn over gloves for special celebrations, leaving the wearer's hand free from encumbrance.

1 Wire up each lily head and bud by cutting the stem quite short and firmly pushing a stub wire through the centre, leaving 10-12cms (4-5ins) of wire with which to join the stems together later. Stem wrap each stem to seal in the moisture and to ensure that the wire stays securely in place. For tips on stem wrapping, see p.62.

Take a metre- (yard-) length of ribbon about 5 or 6cms (2 or 3ins) from the end and make a loop which you hold together at the base. Continue to make loops like this until you run out of ribbon. Wire around the base of the ribbon loop to hold it in position.

Stem wrap the stub wire, leaving at least 8 or 10cms (3 or 4ins) of wire to enable you to attach the ribbon to your corsage. Repeat this process for a second wired loop of ribbon for the other end of the corsage.

2 Take the wired loop of ribbon in one hand, and lay the wired lily bud on top, placing it slightly further down and to one side so as not to obscure the ribbon completely. Stem wrap the two stems together. Position a lily head slightly further down on top of the bud, again taking care not to obscure it completely. Stem wrap onto the main stem.

Putting this wired cluster to one side, repeat the process for the other ribbon loop and lily bud, which will form the second 'half' of the corsage.

Take both halves of the corsage, lay them against each other so that the ribbon loops are pointing in opposite directions and there is no great perceptible gap between the two lily heads. Tie the stem-wrapped wires together in three places (one in the centre, and two near the ends) with the nylon fishing reel. Bend the excess ends of the wire over to make neat loops and to prevent them impaling the wearer. Find the centre of the thin ribbon, tie the ribbon onto the back of the corsage's centre, bind the ribbon around the main wired stem on each side, and tuck the left-hand piece of ribbon through the wire hook at the left end of the corsage. Repeat for the right-hand side. You may want to provide extra security by dotting a touch of glue onto the wire hooks.

The wearer holds the corsage against their wrist, bending the wires gently to the shape. Tie the ends of the two ribbons firmly into a knot and bow, cutting off any excess ribbon.

Arm sheath

LONG TAPERING ARM SHEATHS were also fashionable at this period. These were usually made with longiflorum lilies (otherwise known as bridal or trumpet) or with arum lilies. Often the stems were bound with ribbon, though many photographs of the period show the stems left unbound. This was the precursor of the very stylised arum lily sheath popular in the 1920s.

FLOWERS AND MATERIALS
5 stems longiflorum lilies
6 stems asparagus fern
stem wrap

Starting with the longest stem, work backwards, laying shorter stems of foliage and flowers at 45° angles. These should be placed to the left and right of the first main stem so that the stem ends fan out slightly where they cross the main stem.

Continue to add shorter stems of material until you feel that you have reached the desired length and size of the bouquet. Then bind the stems together firmly with floral tape.

If this is the first time you have made this style of bouquet, you may want to wrap the stems together with floral tape each time you add two or three new stems in order to keep the overall shape under control.

As alternatives, I suggest using orchids, arum or oriental lilies, or long-stemmed, plump-headed roses.

TIPS

It is essential that the pollen stamens are removed from the open lilies to avoid catastrophe (see p.125).

Stem wrapping is always easier if you have warm hands, or you can at least put the tape somewhere to warm it up before you start work. If the tape gets hot, it will just bond together and be unusable.

Wrist corsage bands are available to buy, to cut down on the time it takes to make the arrangement.

Oriental arrangement

FLOWERS AND MATERIALS

3 stems red holme oak
6 twigs
3 stems white oriental lilies
3 stems white arum lilies
oriental style bronze pot
plastic covered chicken wire

THE MYSTERIOUS EAST captured the imagination of our Georgian ancestors, encouraging an enduring fascination with all things oriental (see p.50). Japan, however, remained very much an unknown country until the display of Japanese arts at the International Exhibition in London in 1862, greatly inspiring many artists and designers and providing one strand in the evolution of the Art Nouveau style in the late nineteenth century. Clean, uncluttered lines were reflected in furniture, ceramics and textiles. Designs were influenced by nature, and stylised containers were made in the shape of the lily or tulip, with sinuous curves and crisp, fluid lines.

The fashion for oriental design and craftsmanship, at first considered avant garde, was adopted by a much wider audience in the early twentieth century. Pottery, textiles and furniture were mass-produced to supply the growing demand, in contrast to the honest, simple designs in good quality materials made by proponents of the Arts & Crafts Movement.

Flower arrangements often used a single variety of flowers or plants, although in wealthy households there could be a series of arrangements in the room at one time. These would be displayed on free-standing torchère stands, side tables, desks, mantelpieces and pianos.

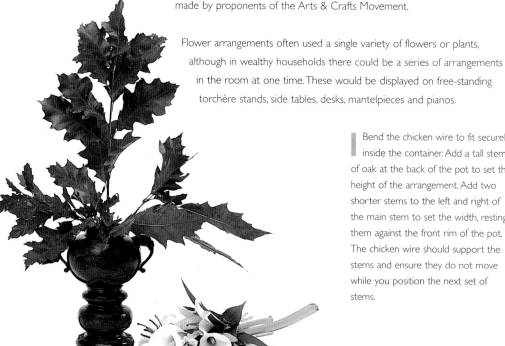

Bend the chicken wire to fit securely inside the container. Add a tall stem of oak at the back of the pot to set the height of the arrangement. Add two shorter stems to the left and right of the main stem to set the width, resting them against the front rim of the pot. The chicken wire should support the stems and ensure they do not move while you position the next set of stems.

ALTERNATIVE ARRANGEMENT

An alternative arrangement using 3 twigs and a large chrysanthemum head in a blue and white porcelain vase.

2 Add the oriental lilies following the outline of the foliage and ensuring that there is a good degree of space between each of the elements. Add the arum lilies in a close spray just off centre of the display. The positioning of the lilies, the main focus in this piece, will draw the eye across the arrangement and imply movement.

3 Add the twigs in the spaces between the foliage to add an overall natural balance to the arrangement.

TIPS

You may want to remove the pollen stamens from the lilies (see p.125).

Top up your vase with water and change the water regularly to prolong the life of the flowers and to avoid stagnant smelling water.

Trumpet vases

FLOWERS AND MATERIALS

3 stems of longiflorum lily *(also
known as the trumpet or Madonna lily)*
3 long stems of asparagus fern
a tall trumpet *(or lily)* vase
sand *(optional)*

LONG, THIN TRUMPET vases became very fashionable in the Edwardian period, fulfilling the desire for simple design incorporating a stylish signature flower. Given their propensity to fall over, these vases were often placed in the corners of rooms or hallways for their protection.

Sand was often added to the bottom of the vase before the water was added, to provide a degree of stability to the arrangement. If using sand, make sure that it has been washed thoroughly, otherwise the water will become very murky.

This arrangement is a typical example of the fashionable style of single variety so highly recommended by the trendsetters of the day, such as Gertrude Jekyll. The style also fulfilled the Arts & Crafts' philosophy of using cut flowers in a manner which was sympathetic to their growth characteristics and habitat. This meant a move towards a more flowing, free style, and away from the fussy, compact shapes of which the Victorians were so fond.

I If you are at all worried about the balance of this arrangement, add a little sand to the bottom of the vase to act as ballast. Then add water so that the vase is three-quarters full.

Hold the lily stems in one hand and arrange them so that there is a tall stem at the back of the arrangement and the other two stems are slightly lower, with one facing more to the right and the other to the left.

Slide all three lily stems into the vase at the same time. This will help to hold them all at the angles mentioned above.

2 Add a tall stem of asparagus fern at the top of the arrangement so that it forms the tallest stem above the tallest lily. Add a stem of fern to the left-hand side of the vase, and the final stem to the right-hand side.

Top the vase up with water until it is full. The vase shown here will hold only 20 fl oz (I pint), so add water every day to ensure that the arrangement does not dry out.

TIPS

To avoid pollen dripping over the petals or your furniture, remember to remove the filaments as they develop. To do this, wait until each flower head is half open and then put your fingers carefully inside the petals and gently pull the hard yellow pollen filaments. These will easily come out and you can throw them away, ensuring that they never create pollen.

If you are unlucky and get pollen on clothing or soft furnishings, don't be tempted to rub with a damp cloth. Instead, double over sticky tape (sticky side out) and gently pat the pollen. You should find that it lifts off the surface of the fabric easily. To remove any last traces, wash the item and hang it in bright sunlight – you should find that the pollen disappears altogether.

Cottage garden arrangement

FLOWERS AND MATERIALS

3 sprays pale pink everlasting pea
5 stems short-stemmed mid-pink
   sweet peas
3 sprays cream hydrangea
3 sprays jasmine
a bowl
a small piece of plastic-coated
   chicken wire
scissors

WHILST MALMAISON carnations, roses, lilies and orchids were the
most popular and stylish flowers for wealthy households, many
Edwardians had an enduring love of the more modest varieties
of flowers traditionally found growing in cottage gardens.

It is during this period that we see a developing trend
for flowers to be used in a style more sympathetic to
the plant's growing characteristics, making use of large
boughs of foliage and long trailing stems of flowers
such as sweet peas and clematis. Short stems wired
into unnatural angles or set into prim, concentric
bands were no longer in fashion.
The effect resulted in a natural
balance between the
container, choice of flowers
and overall style of the
finished decoration.

Fashionable arrangements in unpatterned vases and bowls contained single,
or at most two varieties of flowers, allowing asparagus or maidenhair ferns,
jasmine or gypsophila interspersed to soften the overall effect. This gave a
minimalist feel to flower arranging that did not alter until the 1930s when
Constance Spry transformed the art in her own unique style. In so doing,
she returned to the older tradition of mixing varieties of flowers.

I Remove all lower foliage from the stems and cut ends at a sharp 45° angle so that they can absorb water effectively.

Bend the edges of the chicken wire over so that the cut ends rest against the sides of the bowl to form a base to hold the flower stems in position.

Angle the shortest stem of sweet peas to the left side of the bowl, and then a longer stem slightly lower down on the right-hand side of the bowl. You will now have started to build a lattice of stems beneath the framework of chicken wire to provide even further firm support. Add a tall stem of sweet peas just off centre at the top of the arrangement.

TIPS

Ensure that all the cut stem ends sit well below the waterline of the bowl. Top up the water level every day by placing the fingers of one hand just inside the rim of the bowl

and adding the water with a long-spouted watering can with your other hand. You will feel the water rising and can stop pouring before it reaches the rim of the bowl.

2 Add a spray of hydrangea to the left-hand side of the bowl, repeat with a stem to the right of the central sweet peas, and then add a much shorter stem just off set to the left of the centre at the bottom of the bowl.

Infill using the stems of jasmine and short stems of sweet peas to ensure that none of the chicken wire is visible.

Fireplace decorations

FLOWERS AND MATERIALS

Top Mantle
1 large dragon tree
3 small cyclamen
2 potted chrysanthemums
1 potted aster
4 small ferns
8 short stems aster
6 long stems jasmine foliage
8 stems fern

Fire Hearth
boxes of varying heights to form
   staging if necessary
2 large vases
1 aspidistra
7 house plants
4 small potted ferns
2 potted chrysanthemums
5 potted asters

2 *glass vases of flowers including:*
2 stems hydrangea
2 stems gypsophila
1 stem longhi lily
1 stem pink oriental lily
1 stem yellow oriental lily
1 stem eryngium thistle
1 stem gladiolus
2 stems spray chrysanthemums
1 stem september flowers
1 stem alstroemeria
1 stem snapdragon

THE EDWARDIANS not only displayed vases and pots of flowers on their mantelpieces, but also filled the whole of the inside of the fireplace with large, exuberant arrangements of potted plants and cut flowers. These were set on staging, which was then completely disguised by foliage. Stands were developed to allow the arrangement to be lifted with relative ease out of the fireplace in case a fire needed to be lit unexpectedly. For special occasions, the whole of the mantelpiece could be decorated with an arrangement on a similar or even larger scale.

The arrangement described here reflects the love at this period for cottage garden flowers. Oversize blooms of Malmaison carnations, roses, lilies, orchids and hydrangeas were favourites in the large arrangements. This arrangement could be used as one whole decoration, but the mantelshelf and bottom hearth can be decorated independently, depending on the time of year.

Lay a length of plastic over the mantle to protect it from water damage. Ensure that you place plant saucers of waterproof trays under the plant pots for ease of watering if the arrangement is to last more than one or two days. Place a pair of soaked floral foam blocks in the trays on the mantle. Start to add the potted plants, tallest in the centre, moving down to smaller at the ends.

2 Add a front row of ferns and cyclamen in pots, then disguise these pots by putting your flowers and foliage into the wet foam, working from the outer edges in towards the centre.

If you do not want to use vases of cut flowers in this display, just put a few stems of cut flowers in water phials and push these firmly into the soil of your pots for a splash of colour. Remember to keep the phials topped up with water.

3 Starting on the hearth, cover it with plenty of plastic or a water-proof container. Always use plant saucers to enable you to water the plants adequately. Arrange a row of plants interspersed with the two vases at the back to set the overall height of the display and fill the fireplace completely. You may want to use boxes to get further height for small potted plants. Fill the vases with cut flowers in a natural and loose arrangement, without crushing them together.

4 Add a shorter, second row of pots of plants, keeping a symmetrical balance to the display.

5 Infill a final tier of ferns and small pots of plants to disguise any gaps or glimpses of plant pots.

TIPS

If using a lot of cut flowers and few potted plants, take a large waterproof container with low sides, such as a compost tray or roasting pan, and fill with blocks of wet floral foam in varying heights. The plants can then sit safely on top of the floral foam and the cut flowers and foliage can be kept well watered. Place your hand into the arrangement until you find the top of the foam, then add water carefully with a long-spouted watering can. Move your hand down so that your fingers are just inside the rim of the container, and then you will be able to feel the water rising.

Always make this arrangement in situ, as it would be far too heavy to move easily.

Christmas wreath

FLOWERS AND MATERIALS

3 stems cream carnations
hardy mixed foliage (bay,
    fruiting ivy, holly, conifer,
    Scots pine)
moss or hay
8 gilded pine cones (see p.11)
1 metre (1 yard) burgundy velvet ribbon
1.5 metres (1½ yards) cream satin
    ribbon
a wire wreath frame
reel wire or string
stub wires
scissors
secateurs

THE USE OF WREATHS as decorations for special occasions, festivals and rituals has endured over the centuries. The Edwardians continued this tradition with their own distinctive style.

The era of house parties was in full swing, and no well-dressed door would have been complete without a festive wreath to welcome guests to enter. If real holly berries were in short supply, artificial berries and fruits were always a useful substitute (see p.76).

The new 'freestyle' of arranging flowers meant that fewer, larger blooms could be used instead of a mass of densely-packed, small-headed flowers. Designs made use of focal flowers with soft-textured complementary foliage, and the new philosophy placed as much value on the space between elements of the arrangements as the actual flowers themselves.

Although moss is the traditional material for binding onto wreath frames, a useful alternative is good quality hay. It has many elements in its favour – it is more easily renewable, dry to work with and readily available in small quantities from pet food stores. However, its drawback is that it can be an irritant for anybody with a dust allergy, so always bind the hay onto your base in a well-ventilated area. It can also contain dry, but still prickly, thistles!

Wrap generous amounts of hay or moss over the wire frame, one handful at a time. If using moss or hay, secure it by wrapping the wire loosely around the base and then passing the whole reel through your loose loop. By using this 'blanket stitch' method every few wraps of your wire, you have taken up the tension on the wire and can release your hold without risk of unravelling.

By adding hay/moss to the frame you will bulk it out so that the bunches can be held in place more easily, and the necessary moisture can be retained to keep the finished wreath looking fresh for a longer time. After you have added the last handful of hay/moss, put a final 'blanket stitch' in place, cut the wire and feed the sharp cut end back into the moss to prevent you hurting yourself.

2 Make up small bunches of mixed foliage, leaving a few centimetres (inches) of stems on each bunch to make it easier for you to bind them onto the base. I usually bind a bunch together with a small piece of wire or an elastic band, so that each bunch stays in position while I am working with them. Graduate each bunch with a slightly longer piece of foliage at the back, and shorter pieces on top of this. For a small wire frame you will probably need about six to eight bunches, for a large wreath, twelve to fourteen bunches, although this depends on the length and size of each. It may help to lay each bunch onto the frame as you work so that you can see how many more are required. You can also swap them around until you are happy with the order. When you start to wire them onto the frame you will invariably arrange them more tightly, so don't be surprised if you need an extra bunch at the end.

3 To anchor the bunches securely to the frame, hold the first bunch against the frame and wrap your wire around several times to make the 'blanket stitch' with the reel. Leave your reel attached as you add the next bunch, so that the tips of the foliage cover the stems of the previous bunch, and again make a 'blanket stitch' with your wire.

Continue working around the frame in the same direction without cutting the wire, and angle the bunches slightly to the outside edge of the frame so that you can clearly see the empty hole in the centre. When you get to the last bunch, gently lift the tips of the first bunch and tuck the final bunch into position before making several good 'blanket stitches' to hold it in place. Cut the wire off and feed the cut end into the hay/moss.

Decorate with a sumptuous bow and gilded pine cones (see p.11). To position the bow, push the wire through the foliage and hay/moss and double back the cut end. Add the pine cones to the wreath as you did with the bow, by pushing the wire firmly through the base until it comes out at the back, taking care not to impale yourself, and feed the cut end back into the base.

To make the hanging loop for the wreath, take a hairpin-shaped piece of stub wire and push one leg of this through the base. You need to get this wire through the metal frame rather than just through the outer edge of the hay/moss, so don't put the hanging loop on the very edge of the base. Twist the two legs round each other, feeding the cut ends back into the base.

Finally, soak the wreath in a few centimetres (inches) of water for at least a couple of hours to ensure that the hay/moss is thoroughly wet before giving it pride of place on your front door.

TIPS

To decide which is the top of the wreath, hold it against a door or clear wall surface and rotate until you feel that you have found the best position. If you have a slightly thicker area of foliage, it is preferable to have this at the bottom of the wreath to give the shape better balance. If there is a slight gap between the first and last bunches, this is the good place to put the bow.

If you don't want to hammer a nail into your front door, or have a UPVC door frame, consider investing in a wreath hanger that slots neatly over the top of the door itself. The wreath can then be hung on its integral hook, which shouldn't interfere with the opening and closing of the door. Most wreath hangers will fit even quite thick doors.

If the weather is warm, remember to give the hay/moss base a top up

with water and mist spray the foliage on the front every few days.

If the door is narrow, consider making a smaller-sized wreath and try to avoid prickly foliage which could snag on people as they pass by.

If you live in a rural area and are planning to hang the wreath on an outside gate, avoid using any highly toxic materials such as yew in case livestock are tempted to nibble your precious creation!

ALTERNATIVE ARRANGEMENTS

Wreaths don't just have to be for Christmas.
Here are some seasonal alternatives to decorate
your house for special celebrations

PEONY (LATE SPRING) WREATH

8 stems statice
5 peony flowers
3 peony buds
4 stems pink limonium
6 stems rosemary
6 stems asparagus fern
6 stems variegated ivy
6 stems mid-green ivy
4 stems variegated myrtle

CORNFLOWER AND LILY (SUMMER) WREATH

2 stems pink lilies
16 stems cornflowers
foliage as above

LILY WREATH *(suitable for weddings)*

5 longhi lily heads
1 longhi lily bud
foliage as above
1.5 metres (1½ yards) ivory ribbon
6 sets of crystals on wires
    (available from florists or craft shops)

135

The Language of Flowers

NAME	ASSOCIATION	NAME	ASSOCIATION
Acacia – pink	Elegance, hope, chaste love	Beech	Prosperity
Acacia – yellow	Friendship	Begonia	Beware, dark thoughts
Acanthus	Artifice, the fine arts	Belladonna	Silence
Achillea millefolium	War	Bells of Ireland	Good luck
Aconite (wolfsbane)	Misanthropy	Bindweed (greater)	Insinuation
Aconite (crowfoot)	Lustre	Bindweed (lesser)	Humility
African violet	Such worth is rare	Birch	Meekness
Agapanthus	Love letters	Bittersweet	Truth
Agrimony	Gratitude, thankfulness	Bluebell	Constancy, humility
Alchemilla	Protection	Borage	Courage, cheerfulness
Allspice	Compassion	Box	Firmness
Allspice (berry)	Valuable, precious	Bramble	Remorse, envy, lowliness
Almond blossom	Lover's charm, hopefulness	Broom	Humility
Aloe	Grief	Burnet	A merry heart
Alyssum	Worth above beauty	Buttercups	Cheerfulness, innocence, riches
Amaranth	Fidelity		
Amaranth (globe)	Unfading love, immortality	Calendula	Joy, grief, cruelty in love
Amaryllis	Splendid beauty, pride	Camellia	Beauty, perfection
Ambrosinia	Love returned	Campanula	You are rich in attraction, gratitude
Anemone (field)	Sickness	Chamomile	Energy in adversity
	Sacred Association: Suffering, death	Canary grass	Perseverance
Anemone (garden)	Unfading love, forsaken	Candytuft	Indifference
Angelica	Inspiration	Canterbury bell	Acknowledgement
Aniseed	Restoration of youth, indulgence	Caraway	Steadfast
Apple blossom	Preference	Carnation	Friendship, love, Mother's Day
Arbutus	Thee only do I love		woman's love
Artemisia	Dignity		Sacred Association:
Ash (mountain)	Prudence, intellect		Symbol of the Virgin Mary
Asparagus fern	Secrecy	Carnation –	
Aster	Daintiness, variety	solid colour	Yes
Aster (double)	Reciprocity	Carnation – striped	Refusal
Auricula – scarlet	Avarice	Carnation – yellow	Disdain
Azalea	Temperance	Cactus flower	Warmth
		Catnip	Courage
Basil	Best wishes	Cat's tail	Peace
Bachelor's button	Celibacy, hope in love,	Calceolaria	I offer you my fortune
	single blessedness	Cedar	I live for thee
Balm of Gilead	Sympathy, consolation	Celandine	Joy
Banksia	Love sweet and silent	Chamomile	Patience
Basil	Hatred	Chervil	Sincerity
Bay	Strength, glory, nobility	Chestnut	Do me justice

Associations and meanings have been attached to flowers, herbs and foliage for thousands of years.

The Victorians, however, developed this into a complex language which I have given below.

NAME	ASSOCIATION	NAME	ASSOCIATION
Chicory	Frugality	Daisy (garden)	Innocence, I share your sentiments
Chrysanthemum	Cheerfulness	Daisy (ox-eye)	A token
Chrysanthemum –		Dandelion	Happiness, wishes come true, oracle
red	I love	Daphne	Painted lily, ornament
Chrysanthemum –		Delphinium	Airy
white	Absolute truth, fidelity	Dill	Luck, magical charm
Chrysanthemum –		Dock	Patience
yellow	Slighted love	Dogwood	Durability
Cineraria	Always delightful		
Cinnamon	My fortune is yours	Edelweiss	Noble courage, daring
Clematis	Mental beauty, purity, poverty	Eglantine flowers	Poetry
Clover	Good luck, be mine	Eglantine foliage	Simplicity
Clove	Dignity	Elder	Zealousness
Cockscomb	Foppery, affectation, singularity	Elderflowers	Compassion, consolation
Coltsfoot	Maternal care, justice shall be done	Elm	Dignity
Columbine	Folly	Escallonia	I live for thee
Columbine – purple	Resolution	Eucalyptus	Protection, get well, farewell
Convolvulus	Uncertainty	Eucharis	Maidenly charms
Coreopsis	Constant cheerfulness	Evening primrose	Inconstancy
Coriander	Hidden merit	Everlasting flower	Unfading memories
Corn	Prosperity	Everlasting pea	Wilt thou go with me?
Corncockle	Duration		
Cornflower	Delicacy, refinement	Fennel	Strength, flattery, worthy of all praise
	loyalty, healing powers	Fenugreek	Honey sweet
	Sacred Association:	Fern	Sincerity
	Symbol of the Virgin Mary	Fern (maidenhair)	A secret bond of love
Coriander	Lust	Feverfew	Protection
Cowslip	Winning grace, pensiveness	Fir	Time, elevation
Crocus	Joy, cheerfulness, gladness, abuse not	Fir cone	Order
	Sacred Association:	Flax	Fate, appreciation, domestic virtues
	Symbol of the Resurrection	Fleur-de-lys	Flame
Crown imperial	Arrogance, pride, mourning	Fool's parsley	Silliness
Cumin	Faithfulness	Forget-me-not	Loyalty
Cyclamen	Resignation, goodbye	Forsythia	Anticipation
Cypress	Mourning, death	Foxglove	Insincerity
		French marigold	Jealousy
Daffodil	Respect, regard, chivalry	Fuchsia	Refined taste
	Sacred Association:		
	Resurrection & rebirth, eternal life	Gardenia	Thou art lovely, joy, untold love, peace
Dahlia	Good taste	Garlic	Strength
Daisy	Innocence, simplicity, purity	Gentian	You are unjust

NAME	ASSOCIATION	NAME	ASSOCIATION
Geranium – pink	*Partiality*	Hyacinth – blue	*Constancy, play, sport*
Geranium – rose	*Preference*		*Sacred Assoxiation:*
Geranium – scarlet	*Comfort*		*Death & revival*
Geranium (ivy-leafed)	*I engage you for the next dance, bridal favour*	Hyacinth – purple	*Sorrow*
Geranium (lemon)	*Unexpected meeting*	Hydrangea	*Vanity, heartlessness, boastfulness*
Geranium (nutmeg)	*Expected meeting*	Hyssop	*Protection against evil spirits, sacrifice, cleanliness*
Geranium (scented)	*Melancholy, folly*		
Geranium (silver-leafed)	*Reversed decision*	Indian pink	*Always lovely*
Gillyflowers	*Affectionate bonds, lasting beauty*	Iris	*Faith, authority, victory, wisdom, hope, I have a message for you*
Gladiolus	*Generosity, strong character*	Iris – yellow	*Passionate love*
Gloxinia	*Love at first sight, proud spirit*	Ivy	*Fidelity, friendship, protection against evil spirits*
Golden rod	*Precaution, encouragement*		
Gorse	*Enduring affection*		
Grasses	*Utility*	Jacob's ladder	*Come down*
Gypsophila	*Everlasting happiness, pure of heart*	Japonica	*Love at first sight*
		Jasmine – white	*Extreme amiability, wealth*
Harebell	*Grief*	Jasmine – yellow	*Grace and elegance*
Hawthorn blossom	*Hope*	Jonquil	*Sympathy, affection, I yearn for your affection*
Hazel	*Reconciliation*		
Heartsease	*Remembrance, you occupy my thoughts*	Juniper	*Protection*
Heather – pink	*Good luck*	Kalmia	*Nature*
Heather – white	*Good luck, protection*	Kingcup	*Desire for riches*
Heliotrope	*Devotion*	Knotweed	*Recantation*
Hellebore	*Wards off evil powers, anxiety, scandal, calumny*	Laburnum	*Forsaken*
Hemlock	*You will be my death*	Lady's slipper	*Capricious beauty*
Hibiscus	*Delicate beauty, change*	Lantana	*Vigour*
Hogweed	*Remembrance*	Larch	*Audacity*
Holly	*Defence, foresight, good will*	Larkspur – pink	*Levity, brightness*
Hollyhock	*Female ambition*	Laurel	*Nobility, ambition*
Honesty	*Fascination*	Lavender	*Distrust, devotion, silence, luck*
Honeysuckle	*Generous affection, devotion, rustic beauty*	Lemon	*Purity, virtue, zest*
	Sacred Association:	Lemon balm	*Brings love, longevity, sympathy*
	Lasting pleasures	Lemon blossom	*Fidelity in love*
Hop	*Injustice*	Lemon verbena	*Attracts the opposite sex, delicacy of feelings*
Horehound	*Health*	Lily (calla)	*Beauty*
Houseleek	*Vivacity*	Lily (day)	*Coquetry*

NAME	ASSOCIATION	NAME	ASSOCIATION
Lilac	First love	Narcissus	Self esteem, egotism
Lily (general)	Purity and innocence	Nasturtium	Patriotism, victory in battle, charity
Lily (imperial)	Majesty	Nettle (stinging)	Spite, you are cruel
Lily (Madonna)	Purity	Night scented stock	Devotion
Lily (tiger)	Wealth, pride		
Lily – yellow	Crime	Oak	Hospitality
Lily of the valley	Making the right choice, promise of happiness, sweetness	Oats	Music
		Oleander	Beware
Lime blossom	Conjugal love	Olive	Peace
	Sacred Association: Symbol of the Virgin Mary	Orange	Generosity
		Orange blossom or leaf	Purity, virtue, your purity equals your loveliness
Love-in-a-mist	Love, perplexity		
	Sacred Association: Martyrs		
Love-lies-bleeding	Hopelessness	Orchid	Beauty, love, refinement
Lupin	Voraciousness	Orchid (slipper)	Capriciousness
Magnolia	Dignity, beauty, love of nature	Palm leaf	Victory
Mallow	Ambition, fertility	Pansy	You are in my thoughts
Marigold	Grief, cruelty, jealousy, purity, Sacred Association: The Virgin Mary, affection		Sacred Association: Loyalty, sign of the Holy Trinity
		Parsley	Festivity
Marjoram	Blushes, joy, health & happiness	Pasque flower	You have no claims
Marshmallow	Kindness	Passion flower	Faith
Meadow saffron	Mirth	Peach blossom	Longevity, I am your captive
Meadowsweet	Uselessness	Pennyroyal	Flee away
Michaelmas daisy	Farewell	Peony	Anger, indignation, shame
Mignonette	Your qualities surpass even your charms, excellence		Sacred Association: Mystical powers, an ardent love of God
Mimosa	Sensitivity	Peppermint	Warmth of feeling, cordiality
Mint	Virtue	Periwinkle – blue	Early friendship
Mock orange	Falseness, deceit	Periwinkle – white	Pleasures of memory
Mistletoe	Kiss me, affection, fertility, I surmount all obstacles	Petunia	Never despairing, anger
		Phlox	Sweet dreams, agreement, our hearts are united
Mint	Protection from illness		
Monkshood	Beware, chivalry, fickleness	Pimpernel	Change
Morning glory	Affection	Pine	Hope, pity
Moss	Maternal love, charity, seclusion	Pink	Boldness, love
Mugwort	Happiness	Poinsettia	Cheerfulness
Myrtle	Love enduring, Love in absence, love	Polyanthus	Pride of riches
		Poplar	Courage

NAME	ASSOCIATION	NAME	ASSOCIATION
Poppy	*Imagination, eternal sleep*	Rose (wild)	*Simplicity*
Poppy – red	*Pleasure*	Rosebud – pink	*Perfect happiness, you are young and beautiful*
	Sacred Association:		
	The Eucharist, Christ's Passion	Rosebud – white	*Love, ignorance of love*
Poppy – white or field	*Consolation*	Rosebud – yellow	*Friendship*
Poppy – yellow	*Wealth*	Rosemary	*Remembrance, rue, remorse, repentance*
Prickly pear	*Satire*		
Primrose	*Young love*		*Sacred Association:*
Primrose (evening)	*Inconstancy*		*Love evergreen, death*
Primrose – red	*Unpatronized merit*		
Primula	*Contentment, thoughtlessness*	Saffron	*Marriage*
	Sacred Association:	Sage	*Wisdom, long life, esteem, domestic virtue*
	Symbol of Christ's Resurrection, flower of compassion		
		Salvia – blue	*I think of you*
		Salvia – red	*Energy, forever thine*
Quaking grass	*Agitation*	Scabious	*Unfortunate love*
Quince	*Temptation*	Scilla – blue	*Forgive & forget*
		Smilax	*Loveliness*
Ranunculus	*Radiant charms*	Snapdragon	*No, presumption*
Rhododendron	*Beware*	Snowdrop	*Hope, consolation*
Rose (gallica)	*Joy, love*	Sorrel	*Affection*
	Sacred Association:	Southernwood	*Jesting, merriment*
	Dedicated to the Virgin Mary	Spearmint	*Warmth of sentiment*
Rose – black	*Death*	Speedwell	*Fidelity*
Rose – dark crimson	*Mourning*	Statice	*Lasting beauty*
Rose – deep red	*Bashful love*	Star of Bethlehem	*Sacred Association:*
Rose – red and white together	*Unity, blood and bandages*		*Atonement*
		Stephanotis	*Happiness in marriage*
Rose – white	*I am worthy of you*	Stock	*Promptness, everlasting beauty*
Rose – yellow	*Jealousy, declining love*	Strawberry	*Modesty, perfect goodness, fertility, abundance*
Rose (cabbage)	*Ambassador of love*		
Rose (China)	*Beauty always new*		*Sacred Association:*
Rose (damask)	*Brilliant complexion, freshness*		*Purity & sensuality*
Rose (dog)	*Pleasurable but painful love*	Sunflower	*Loyalty, haughtiness, adoration*
Rose (full bloom)	*Gratitude*		*Sacred Association:*
Rose (leaf)	*You may hope*		*Devotion to the Catholic Church*
Rose (moss)	*Superior merit*	Sweet basil	*Good luck*
Rose (musk)	*Capricious beauty*	Sweet cicely	*Gladness*
Rose (rambler)	*Only deserve my love*	Sweet pea	*Goodbye, departure, lasting pleasure*
Rose (tea)	*I will always remember*	Sweet William	*Gallantry, a smile*
Rose (thornless)	*Love at first sight*	Sycamore	*Curiosity*

NAME	ASSOCIATION	NAME	ASSOCIATION
Tamarisk	*Crime*	Zinnia	*Thoughts of friends*
Tansy	*Hostile thoughts*	Zinnia – yellow	*Daily remembrance*
Teasel	*Misanthropy*		
Thistle	*Austerity*		
Thorn branch	*Severity*		
Thrift	*Sympathy*		
Thyme	*Courage, strength*		
Tuberose	*Dangerous pleasures*		
Tulip – red	*Wealth & importance, declaration of love*		
Tulip – yellow	*Hopeless love*		
Valerian	*Readiness, accommodating disposition*		
Verbena	*Enchantment*		
Veronica	*Fidelity*		
Vervain	*Enchantment*		
Vine	*Intoxication*		
Violet – blue	*Humility, modesty, faithfulness in love* *Sacred Association: The humility of the Virgin Mary*		
Violet – white	*Modesty, innocence*		
Viscaria	*Will you dance with me?*		
Wallflower	*Fidelity in adversity*		
Water lily	*Pure heart*		
Wheat	*Prosperity*		
Willow	*Mourning*		
Wisteria	*I cling to you, welcome, regret*		
Witch hazel	*A spell*		
Woodbine	*Fraternal love*		
Woodruff	*Sweet humility*		
Wood sorrel	*Joy*		
Wormwood	*Absence*		
Xeranthemum	*Cheerfulness under adversity*		
Yarrow	*Healing, foretelling the future*		
Yew	*Sorrow*		

Select Bibliography

Ashelford, Jane, *The Art of Dress: Clothes and Society 1500-1914,* 1996

Beeton, Mrs Isabella, *The Book of Household Management,* 1861 and
    later editions

Blacker, Mary Rose, *Flora Domestica,* 2000

Blunt, Wilfred, *Tulipomania,* 1950

Burbidge, F.W.T., *Domestic Floriculture,* 1874

Campbell-Culver, Maggie, *The Origin of Plants,* 2001

Cole, Herbert, *Heraldry and Floral Forms as used in Decoration,* 1922

Conder, Josiah, *The Flowers of Japan and the Art of Floral Arrangement,* 1891

Davies, Jennifer, *The Victorian Flower Garden,* 1991

Earle, Mrs. C.W., *Pot Pourri from a Surrey Garden,* 1897

Felton, Robert, *British Floral Decoration,* 1910

Fisher, Louise B., *An Eighteenth Century Garland*

Furber, Robert, *The Flower Garden Display'd,* 1734 (second edition)

Gerard, John, *Herball or Generall Historie of Plantes,* 1597

Girouard, Mark, *Life in the English Country House,* 1978

Hibberd, James Shirley, *Rustic Adornments for Homes of Taste,* 1856

Kent, Elizabeth, *Flora Domestica or The Portable Flower Garden,* 1823

Garnett, Oliver, *Living in Style,* 2002

Hassard, Annie, *Floral Decorations for Dwelling Houses,* 1875

Jekyll, Gertrude, *Home and Garden,* 1900

Jekyll, Gertrude, *Flower Decoration in the House,* 1907

Maling, Miss, *Flowers for Ornament and Decoration and how to
    arrange them,* 1862

March, T. C., *Flower and Fruit Decoration,* 1862

Paston-Williams, Sara, *The Art of Dining,* 1993

Perkins, John, *Floral Decorations for the Table,* 1877

Smith, Georgiana, *Table Decoration,* 1968

Terry, Henry, *A Victorian Flower Album,* 1978

Thornton, Peter, *Seventeenth Century Interior Decoration
    in England, France and Holland,* 1983

Index